OUTSPOKEN
THE MEMOIR

OUTSPOKEN

THE MEMOIR

CEDRIC **THORBES**

Printed in the United States of America
Keen Vision Publishing, LLC
www.keen-vision.com
ISBN: 978-1-948270-80-9

For my very first friend, mentor, and guiding light, my mother,
Loretta Lynn Warren

CONTENTS

ODE TO MOM

On February 9th
I met the love of my life
The way we cuddled and hugged just symbolized love
She told me she would love me for eternity
When her hair turned grey, beauty went away with a face
full of wrinkles on display
She said she would never change
How some would come and go
To and fro
She said she would remain the same
She loved me before she knew my name
In all reality
She loved me before she knew my personality
Before she knew my characteristics
She would listen to me all the times I could not even say it
Made me the winner of the game and shouted my name
when I did not even know how to play it
Deleting things from my mind from time to when I could
not even erase it
She said

I cannot teach you everything
But I can show the basics
And the rest, I guess you'll just have to take it
So just to do you right
The love of my life
Everything I want
I have to chase it
She has my back 100%
She was my comprehension when I could not understand it
Gave me a place to be safe even during times when I felt
abandoned
Kept me in pocket when like Vick, I was scrambling
Took the bullets out of my firearm, so even when I bust
shots, I did no harm
Even when I went on a rampage on my bad days, she
brought me back to calm
Never intentionally treating me wrong
The only person when in times in my life when I cried all
night
She held me in her arms
Always made me feel protected
And every verbal beating was hectic but at the same time a
blessing, so I had no choice but to respect it
She knows me better than I know myself
Loving me unconditionally through sickness and through
health
Through poverty and to wealth
Through situations I cannot even help
She taught me to play spades so I could learn to deal with
the hand that I was dealt

My mother was always different though
Only girl in the world I wanted to kiss on the cheek under
the mistletoe
Put her hand over my mouth before I let my verbal missiles
go
Always brought me back down to earth
When I thought I was too grown to pay attention
Not to mention
Without her, I'm like a car with no engine
With a blown out suspension
With no purpose in fixing
Always told me that if it was too hot then to get out of the
kitchen
But sometimes burned because I was too hard-headed to
listen
Her beauty is unmatchable
Her flow of love, care, and hope is magical
Through cries and laughter
Even the moments after
Had me outside of wedlock but still unconditionally loved
this bastard
And I am grateful for every lesson
  To my mother: peace, prosperity, and blessings

All I need is a sheet of paper and something to write with,
and then I can turn the world upside down.

Friedrich Nietzsche

PART ONE

FAMILY MATTERS

I remember walking downstairs into the kitchen and seeing Tiffany sitting at the table. Her head was down, the lights were dim, but she was focused. I stood there silently for a moment, watching her close enough to be nosy but not close enough for her to notice my presence. Tiffany was the true definition of a Tomboy. She wore baggy clothes and rarely did anything with her hair. She hung with the boys, dressed like the boys, played with the boys, and fought like the boys. Heck, a lot of the time, she fought even better. Tiffany was more of a boy than most of the guys I knew growing up in the hood. She was rough and the last thing I wanted to do was disturb her and make myself a target on one of her many warpaths.

If you have not guessed it by now, Tiffany is my loving, older sister. Even though she is as stubborn as an ox and as vicious as two pit bulls locked in a cage together — she is a genuine, free-spirited person who taught me just about everything I know about being a young man. She taught me the value of compassion — that I should never look down on others and their situations. She taught me how to defend myself in a place where it was either be tough or be constantly ridiculed by your peers. I also thank her for my sense of style. Although many of my clothes were hand-me-downs from my older brother and sister, Tiffany taught me how to care for what I had. She taught me how to clean my sneakers with soap, a toothbrush, and a cup of water so they would last longer. Tiffany showed me how to wear my clothes, so I looked cool and would not get picked on by the kids in my neighborhood. From time to time, she would even buy my clothes because my mother did not have enough cash to provide for everyone in the house. Constant teasing matches between the boys and girls in the neighborhood would always keep you on your toes about your appearance. You never wanted to be ousted for not keeping up with the trends. That was always the irony about growing up in the hood. Many families did not have much, but we always wanted to make sure we looked like we had more than others. We were financially poor, but we were a proud poor and took pride in how we looked.

At the age of 11, I began working small odd jobs. I got paid under the table for washing cars and sweeping gas station parking lots around the city. My mother would never take any of the money I earned. I used it to buy what I needed for the upcoming school year and any clothing my mother could not afford.

Once we hit a certain age, my mother no longer tried to hide the fact that she was low on money. Although I did not know the true severity of our financial situation, I knew at certain times, hunger would greet me at my doorstep. At certain times, rooms normally lit by fluorescent light bulbs would hold the dim flicker of a candle. At certain times, the house would be warmed by a heated stove with the door ajar for maximum impact. I knew at certain times, eviction would cause us to be forced out of our home to seek refuge with my grandparents. I knew at certain times, I could not get what I wanted. It wasn't because my mother didn't want to buy it for us — she simply couldn't. I guess our financial situations did not seem so bad because all of the children in our neighborhood were familiar with those "certain times." We all pretty much lived the same. Some kept their homes cleaner than others, but we all pretty much had the same things. My mother would say to us, "If it is something you want, you have to go and work for it because I cannot afford it." Tiffany always worked several jobs to make sure she stayed in the freshest gear. I guess we could say I got my go-getter mentality from my sister, too. She was always trying to figure out the next move. She did not always do what made the most sense, but she always did what made the most cents instead.

For a little black boy growing up in the hood, my sister addressed all essential needs for survival. Though sometimes cruel, her lessons prepared me for a life outside of my home. Successfully maneuvering through life might have been difficult if it were not for her antics. Of everything Tiffany passed down to me, I am most grateful to her for teaching me to love literature and writing. It was never anything she said — it was what she did that set the example.

Tiffany would sit around for hours at a time, writing anything that came to her mind. She would write short stories, books, poems, raps — two or three at a time — and she was good. We had a Gateway desktop computer we used to download instrumentals from a site called LimeWire. Our mother often scorned us because some of the downloads would give the computer a serious virus that required hundreds of dollars and hours to correct. Even after being warned of a potential beating, my sister took her chances anyway. She would pick a beat, start freestyling, and I would watch. I tried to hop in every now and again to show my skills — or the lack thereof at this point in my life.

After a while, we convinced our mom to buy us a CD-Burner. We would download the instrumentals to the computer and transfer them to a blank CD. This was a time before music could be downloaded directly to your phone and accessible in a matter of seconds. The songs had to be downloaded, placed in a zip file, transferred to the disc, and extracted from the zip file. It was tough work. When all the labor was done, you finally put the CD in a CD Player and listen to the music. When my mother bought me an all grey Sony Walkman, I carried it around religiously. Getting this Walkman was a pivotal point for me for three reasons:

1. It kept us out of trouble with our mother for hogging the living room all day.
2. It allowed me to take the CD's with instrumentals into my room and practice my raps without judgment.
3. Since I could now take my music with me, it allowed me to practice all of the time, not just in the house.

Although my sister indulged in many different forms of writing, I was always most impressed with her raps and poems. Her style was raw and aggressive. Her cadence was uptempo, and between the wordplay and metaphors, I could not get enough. Her aggressive approach and delivery always stuck out because it was different from most female rappers or poets I heard. She did not talk about love, going on dates, or the blue midnight sky. She talked about real life and, more importantly, the lifestyle we had grown accustomed to living in the hood. Needless to say, it rubbed off on me, and I fell in love with the idea of telling the stories of my people.

Before I could even gather the courage to speak what I had written on my pad (it was not good anyway), I had several others who influenced my style & presentation. Although these individuals were not MC's themselves, they introduced me to a world I would often use to escape the real calamities in my life. They introduced me to real hip hop, R&B, and Neo-Soul. This was back when rap was rap and lyrics actually mattered.

Growing up, my Uncle Barry was the coolest person I knew. He was a military man and stood about 5'11, 200 lbs. He had dark bronze skin, always kept a clean-shaven face, and was built like a G.I. Joe action figure. He looked good, always smelled good, and dressed the part. My uncle was far from rich, but he was the most successful person in our immediate family. During my adolescence, he played a huge role in my life as a father figure, due to the absence of my biological father. I am not sure where my biological father was. I had seen a seldom photo or two of him, but outside of those instances, my father was a stranger to me. If I saw him on the street, I would have probably looked him in his face, shook his hand, but would not be able to identify him, or his likeness. My mother never talked about my father. For most of my life, until I became an adult, his presence merely did not exist. As a child, the absence of my father did not harm me one way or the other.

I loved it when my uncle and cousin picked up my older brother, Curtis, and I on the weekends and took us to the movies. It was our "guy time." I am pretty sure my brother and cousin wanted to see the movies. For me, it was something else. Do not get me wrong; the movies and lunches were cool. But more than anything, I liked riding in my uncle's truck listening to music. In the back of that white Ford Explorer, I got schooled on all of the greats: Jay-Z, Nas, Biggie Smalls, Kanye West, A Tribe Called Quest, Big Daddy Kane, and Slick Rick — real Hip Hop! You name it; he had it. I loved listening to those artists because they each had their own style. Each artist was unique in their sound, delivery, rhythm, and flow. Each artist had only one commonality — they were storytellers, providing us with a view of the world from their lenses, neighborhoods, and family experiences.

I would listen to this music for hours at a time. Many of my days would be consumed with rap lyrics from music I was eager to learn. I wanted to know the words to every popular song on the radio. I would sing and dance around the house, making obnoxiously loud noises. I had even begun to make my own lyrics, prance around, and do strange movements with my body as my older siblings would pound and make beats on the table to urge me on. I loved the way music made me feel. When I heard a good tune, I came alive, infused with the passion I had to express. As I rapped all of the lyrics to the songs, even the ad-libs, I was in my most congenial state.

Whenever I speak with my uncle, I often thank him for

providing me with such a great taste in music and introducing me to the true storytellers of the craft. In America, we call them rappers. In my circle, they would be known as griots, and that is how I like to refer to them.

Although I had already begun to write various rhymes on my pad and share verses with my sister in the house, I still did not fully understand the craft - what it meant to have a course, write a bar, and why 16 bars are considered a full verse. All of this changed when I heard Jay-Z's The Black Album. It was the first time I listened to a whole CD all the way through without skipping a song. The album was fearless, blunt, complex, and lyrically sound. It was urban, and it was political. Jay-Z did his thing. His flow and cadence made the music seem as if it were acted out in front of me like a stage play. Each line depicted his life and journey from growing up in Brooklyn to making it big time. His conviction made me feel like I was with him in every moment. I felt his words and stories as if they were my own because of its relatability. I, too, wanted to make it big time. If only I could figure out how Jay-Z got it done, I often thought. I began to study the rappers I idolized. I had to know everything about them — where they were from, their age, and what got them interested in music.

The Black Album was a perfect balance, and I wanted my flow balanced in the same way. I did not want to sound like Jay-Z, but I did like his approach to the music. I wanted to be intriguingly complex - full of metaphors and similes while still providing content containing substance. After this album, I knew for sure I did not just want to write these stories and experiences; I wanted to be skilled enough to tell them my way. So I began to practice my raps every day from sunup to sundown — except on Saturdays.

Saturday mornings at my mother's house were not just for cartoons & cereal. They were also for deep cleaning. Scrubbing tubs, toilets, floors, walls, and counters were essential parts of the weekend routine. The smell of PineSol, Fabuloso, and bleach would always determine what type of Saturday it would be. Weekend cleanups were in addition to the weekly chores list already posted on the fridge. The difference? This was a supervised cleaning, which meant there were no shortcuts, and you would be there until you did the job correctly.

At the top of the morning, my mother would barge into our rooms one by one and demand everyone to get out of bed. She would line us up and give each of us several tasks to complete for the day. I was often tasked with cleaning the bathroom and vacuuming the carpeted areas of the house. I was not allowed in the kitchen for a while because my mother insisted the dishes were not being properly washed. I hated cleaning the kitchen, and if half-doing it would result in me not having to do it at all, I was definitely down for the half-doing. Eventually, my mom caught on to my antics, and I was forced back to the kitchen. This time around, my mom made me a promise to ensure I did my best work.

The one positive thing about Saturday morning cleaning was my mother would play soulful music, which helped pass the time. The likes of Jill Scott, Erykah Badu, Floetry, and Angie Stone echoed throughout the house, creating a sense of peace during our morning routine. Songs like Bag Lady and Long Walk had everyone working in sync like an assembly line. Thanks to my mom, Neo-Soul music became my second love. As I began to write more and more, these artists provided an alternative to the Hip-Hop that consumed my life.

For a short time, I wrote raps just about every single day. I wrote raps on the way to and from school. I wrote raps in the car on my way to the store. I traded in my outdoors time with friends to practice my raps. I always had a pen to write with and something to write on. I would write on just about anything you could think of —notepads, paper bags, or paper towels — to catch my thoughts in the moment. These thoughts turned into bars; the bars turned into verses; the verses turned into songs. I had a composition book full of raps, and I would memorize them, line for line.

Although I was not big time, I was making a name for myself as one of the best rappers in the neighborhood. Back in 2004-2005, when I began to take rap seriously, so did everyone else. Just about anyone you could think of wanted to be a rapper. This gave me ample time to practice my skills because there was a cypher going on anywhere you went. We would huddle up in groups of 10-15 people — just enough folks to have a few rappers, a DJ, and a decent crowd. The DJ would either play a beat, beatbox, or make a beat on a table, depending on the setting. The rhymes would flow from there. I always seemed to capture the crowd's attention when it was my turn. Each of my punchlines was followed by oohs and ahhs. Each cypher would finish with people dapping me up and telling me how good they thought I was. It made me feel pretty good about myself and gave me the encouragement I needed to keep writing.

I vividly remember when I got into my first rap battle. I had participated in many cyphers before, but never in a rap battle. In a cypher, everyone jumps in, raps their verse, and steps back out of the circle. In a rap battle, you versus another person, going verse for verse until ultimately, someone loses. Although we never outwardly distinguished a winner and loser, you could tell who won by the crowd's reactions. Let's just say for the first time I could remember, I was not the crowd favorite.

The cypher started as normal. Everyone stood around, nodding their heads, swaying their bodies, and listening to the beat. When I stepped in the cypher, I was greeted with compliments and cheers from those observing. I caught the beat and proceeded to say:

If ya scared of the future pass it back to me
You boys are dead just like an old battery
I hold heavy metal just like a factory
Head of what I do, CEO of the company
Headed out to dinner, you dudes were lunch to me
Ate 'em up 12 o'clock noon just brunch to me
Never slip, fly chick will accompany me
My watch face looks sort of like a compass piece
Better than half these others rappers
Wanna step to Cedric, man, these dudes is half backward
Trying to end your career earlier your half backwards
When it comes to competition there's just laughter
I ain't wor-

Then it happened. Darnell walked into the cypher, cut me off mid-sentence, and started rapping. I was astonished because, until that point, no one had ever interrupted me during my turn in a cypher. I was infuriated. The nerve of this guy to intervene during my moment. The crowd loved every minute of it. They oohed, ahhed, and cheered him on. So I stood down and shared the space.

His delivery was slow, and his style was more comedic and unorthodox. Initially, I nodded my head as Darnell caught the beat. Then, as I started to hear his words and see the crowd's reactions, I realized he was talking about me. And he talked about me pretty good.

Darnell's raps were not about how good his flow was, how tough he was, what he had, or where he was from. His raps were more about jokes and making people laugh. I will be honest; the raps were not so good. But he talked about me so bad, everyone laughed at me as he stole the crowd. Although his raps were not serious, you could tell he took his craft seriously. You could tell he practiced. You could tell he worked on his cadence and style. You could tell at that moment, he wanted to be seen as the best. He simply felt he was better, and on that day, he proved he was.

Although time would pass and I would battle Darnell several other times and come out victorious, the first battle taught me several important lessons about life. The first was to always be prepared. Although we cannot predict every situation that will occur, prepare as best as possible. There is a saying that goes, "Piss poor preparation leads to a piss poor performance." I began to live by the mantra, "Stay prepared so you do not have to get prepared." The second lesson I learned was that life is competitive. In order to be great, you have to constantly compete with something, even if that something is yourself. The willingness to continuously push yourself to learn new ideas, strategies, and techniques will always keep you ahead of the competitive curve. As things change, we must constantly reinvent ourselves to stay relevant and successful. Lastly, I learned to trust the work put in. Always believe you are good enough and have what it takes to be successful in any situation. It is simply not enough for others to think you are good and know your potential. You have to know your potential and believe it for yourself. More than anything in this world, believe in who you are, and know that what you bring to the table is beyond good enough.

Reflecting upon that time, I can say I did not feel confident in myself when Darnell challenged me. Although I liked to rap and took it seriously, I appreciate that situation because it made me want to be competitive. It transformed rap from being something I did for fun into something I obsessed over. I wanted to be good. And when I say good, I wanted to be better than everyone else. In fact, I had gotten so good I was invited to my first studio session.

A local rapper who knew my older sister heard some of my raps and inquired if I would be interested in coming with him to the studio. He told Tiffany he wanted to do a song with me, and he would allow me additional time to record some music of my own. Of course, when Tiffany told me where we were going to the studio, I was more than excited. I had never been to a studio before, and I always wanted to know how it felt. I always heard the famous rappers talking about it, and I felt this was my chance to prove myself.

This was a dream for me. For a while, I had been making songs and recording them on my MP3 player. Once again, technology had not reached the level of advancement we see now. However, the MP3 was an upgrade from my Walkman, so I was grateful.

When we arrived at the studio, it was not the plush state of the art facility I envisioned in my mind. It was a small makeshift studio placed in the corner of a basement in someone's house. A simple Pro Tools kit and a stand-alone microphone that hid behind a curtain were designated as the studio area. It was not the biggest stage, but the lights were on, and it was time to perform. I waited for about 30 minutes before it was my turn to step in the booth. I will be honest, I was nervous, but as soon as I heard the beat through the headphones and started rapping, all of the butterflies went away, and I felt at home. I recorded three songs in about 25 minutes. I only needed one take on each. I did a second recording to be layered on top of the first during the mixing stage. The studio owner said I was a natural. The artist who invited us to the studio liked my music more than his own. I did not get a reaction from my sister until we got in the car. She never said it was good, but she played it loudly in the car the whole ride home. I knew she was vibing with the music when I caught her nodding her head heavily to the songs.

We did not get home until later in the evening, so I had to wait until the next day to play the songs for my mother. I was so proud of what I accomplished, and I was eager to see my mom's reaction. The next day, my sister and I called my mom into the living room and played the songs for her. My mother had never heard me rap seriously. If you were to ask my mother her version of this story, she would say she did not know I was rapping at all. Regardless of the version, she was impressed. She did not like all the cursing she heard, but she recognized my skills and applauded them. She instantly demanded a personal copy of the CD and played it for all of her friends. She was so proud. Even to this day, I believe she hoards that CD and plays it whenever she misses me.

I am always thankful for the belief my mother and family have in me. No matter what I decided to do, they have always been my biggest supporters. In this situation, it was no different. After making a mixtape, I knew two things:

1. I was good at rap, and other people thought so too.
2. Writing made me happy, although I had not yet realized all of its true benefits.

PART TWO

MY OWN WORST ENEMY

In the summer of 2007, I had to attend summer school because my 8th-grade academic performance was far from stellar. Honestly, I should have been retained based on the amount and quality of work I produced. My final year of middle school ended with a 0.9 GPA. I had all F's and one A — the A was in Physical Education. However, due to my high performance on the standardized state test, I was pushed along to 9th grade under the stipulation that I completed summer school.

Summer school lasted several weeks and required me to take a few English and Math courses. It was the equivalent of a regular school day, except we were dismissed a few hours earlier. Although this school was on a different side of town and had completely different students, students' activities were all the same. We laughed, cracked jokes, and goofed off when time permitted. During lunch, we rapped.

"Congratulate the champion and welcome to violence
In silence, I'm the man to be the spark of the riot
I'm fire
I'll probably be the torch to your flame

And if my word is like that crack, then put the needle to vein
My flow is off the brain
You should call it insane
In this game, I leave you melting like a candle when flamed
I'm the shit, so put the tissue under my name
And boys get scuffed like Nikes when I'm creeping Main
My record is flawless, no losses when I step on the plain
And I'm fly like I just stepped off of a plane
And it's easy
Trust and believe me
I devour a coward like a sandwich because I'm greedy
Truth be told, I'm past cold
Man, I'm freezing
Somewhere in the arctic so the boys who wanted to start me could
not reach me
I'm always on like your TV
Lights, camera, action
Flows hit hard I make you stumble backward"

Rapping was always my "way in" when I got to new places. Do not get me wrong; I was a cool dude. Most people would speak to me, and I would become popular amongst friends. Yet, what always took it over the top was when people found out I could rap. I instantly became a favorite at summer school. All of the teachers and most of the students knew my name and that I was the boy who out-rapped everyone in the cafeteria. The staff even asked me to perform at one of the events they hosted for summer school students. I would ultimately decline for several reasons; however, I was flattered that they asked.

I finished summer school being very popular amongst peers and with A's in all of my classes. I had done just enough to make it to the 9th grade. My mother was furious because she felt I wasted my summer. She knew I could have been making A's all along. She insisted I wasn't applying myself, and she was right. Nonetheless, I feel the learning experience taught me a lot about myself. When I applied myself, I could do just about anything successfully. I simply had to put in the work. In this situation, the work was done, and I was moving to the next chapter of my life — high school.

I sat by the door, waiting for the mailman at my grandmother's house. Each year, the school district would mail out enrollment letters to tell parents of the incoming freshman class which high school their child would be attending. High school selections were normally based on geographic location and middle school placements, with some exceptions.

There were two high schools in my area, East High School and Glenville High School. East High was located on E. 71 Street on Superior Avenue and Glenville on E. 113th Street, right off St. Clair. Both on Cleveland's Eastside. I prayed I would be selected to attend Glenville like it was the only thing I ever wanted. Glenville was known for its excellent athletic programs, and all the while I was rapping, I was also an aspiring athlete - just like every boy my age growing up in the inner city. Besides, all of my family went to Glenville. It was sort of a Rights of Passage in my house. My mother, sister, brother, aunt, uncle, and many of my cousins all attended Glenville High School. It was only right that I continue the family legacy. My best friend, Big Rob, had been enrolled there, so, of course, I hoped to be enrolled at Glenville too.

One blistering hot day in July, I was outside playing curb ball with my friends, and the mailman came. School was getting ready to start in a few weeks, and I had yet to receive my enrollment letter. Something told me today would be the day. I stopped the game immediately and ran across the street to meet the mailman at the door. This particular mailman had been servicing my grandparents' neighborhood for years. As of today, I do not recall his name, but I know I did make him aware of my eagerness to receive this letter several days prior. When I reached him at the doorstep, he handed me a stack of envelopes and said to me, "I think I have what you've been waiting for." At the very top of the pile, a letter from Cleveland Municipal School District (CMSD).

I dashed upstairs into my grandparents' house and rushed to the kitchen table. We were not currently living at our grandparents' house, but we never changed the address after we moved out. My mother did not want me to have to leave my friends and change schools again. We moved around a lot, and my grandparents' house was the one stable place in our lives. I sat down at the table, took the letter off the top, and gave the remainder of the mail to my grandmother. I stared at the letter for a moment. Then, I ripped it open. The letter read, "Your scholar, Cedric Thorbes, will be attending East High School." in bold print. I nearly passed out. No, No, No! How could this happen to me? I was beyond disappointed. I did not want to go to East High. In my heart, I felt I was to be a Glenville Tarblooder, and the thought of having to go to any other school just gave me an uneasy feeling. I'm not sure why I felt this way, but I did. When I got home, I immediately let my mother know about it. I told her I could not envision myself going to East High and knew I would hate it there. I requested she put in a transfer for me to attend Glenville before the school year started. Thankfully, she did. Attending Glenville turned out to be one of the best things for me. Looking back, all of the fighting I did really did not matter. By the time I graduated from high school, East High was a part of Glenville, anyway. But, that's another story, for another book, on another day.

The first day of high school finally rolled around, and although very excited, I was nervous as a pig at a hog roast. High school was a whole new challenging adventure, and I had no idea what to expect. At my middle school, there were a total of about 500 students. At Glenville, the school held around 2000 students, 900 of whom were part of my freshmen class. Most of my neighborhood friends went to East High School, so I initially did not have many friends. It was just my boy Big Rob and I. My brother, Curtis, and a few of my cousins were already attending Glenville, however, they would not speak to me because I was an underclassman. I knew that even without their help, if I remained myself, I would be fine.

The school building wasn't anything impressive. It was an old, three-story brick structure built in 1964. Each floor had an identical design with the same old blue lockers and beige perforated walls on each hall. There were a large auditorium and gymnasium on the first floor and a lecture room on the third floor. This is where I would spend most of my freshman year as the 3rd floor was designated for 9th graders. The rule was, "If you were not a freshman, you were not to be on the third floor, and if you were a freshman, you shouldn't be on any other floor." The only exception was lunchtime when we had to travel to the first floor to go to the cafeteria. The commotion around lunchtime allowed us to intermingle with the upperclassmen and sneak off into other parts of the building. I never snuck out of the cafe to go to other floors. After I developed some new friends and reconnected with a few old ones, we sat in the back of the cafeteria and freestyled. If ever the opportunity presented itself, and I felt the challenge was worthy, I would always intervene.

"Back to business like a champion
I'm flyer than you'll ever be
So much green in my pocket I can make a money tree
Bumblebee
Yeah, the flows sting, and it's poisoning
But the way you bow ya head to ya boy is humbling
Crumbling
Any competition that's in front of me
Throw a stack up and watch it rain like its thundering
Honestly, name another cat who can get with me
My words are like proverbs
The Lord says it's the gift in me
Cooking up dope flows
The wrist work, and I got the recipe
All about my Nikes' signs, so ain't nobody checking me
Keep it cool because my big homie he a shooter like Pistol Pete
I'm the greatest on this mic fam, gone head and face defeat"

By the time I reached my freshman year of high school,

my rap catalog had improved tremendously. I had come into my own with rapping, and at the age of 13, my skills were serious. I had been to the studio several times since the first, collaborated with various artists, made several new songs, expanded my vocabulary, and my freestyle/battle rapping skills were tight. I was confident in what I brought to the table, and I was ready for whatever the next level of high school had to offer. Awful enough, what I had to offer high school at the time had nothing to do with scholastics.

School wasn't a big priority during that time of my life. If you were to ask 13-year-old Cedric, he was focused on other things. As I reflect on my life, I would say I was not focused on anything at all. Although I was rapping my life away, I did not have any actual goals for high school or my life. I was taking it day by day. My lack of aspiration would ultimately leave me falling by the wayside.

Despite the fact I wasn't applying myself in school, I wasn't a trouble maker or a disrespectful student. Even though I wasn't serious about getting my education, I was not the type of person to disrupt a classroom and prevent another person from getting theirs. I have never cursed out a teacher or threw things around the classroom. My mom did not tolerate her children disrespecting adults. One time in middle school, I was disrespectful to a teacher. After refusing to do work in my English class, my teacher threatened me with detention. I scolded her, smacked my lips, and looked her up and down. I did not say a word, but I put on my hood and laid my head on the desk. She called for me again, and I ignored her. She then threatened to call my mother, to which I proceeded to look up at her, give her two big thumbs up, and a humorless smile. I then returned my head to the desk, face down. When I returned home from school that evening, I was greeted by a fury of fists and my mother's belt. She beat me all around the house until she felt I understood the gravity of my actions. I ran, jumped, hollered, hid, and screamed to no avail. She was on me and demanded I apologize to my teacher the next day. My teacher did not deserve disrespect, but I was humiliated. I had to apologize in front of the same class I had been so tough in front of the previous day. I guess I wasn't so tough after all. After a beating of such caliber, I never disrespected a teacher in any manner again.

I was a student some academic behaviorists would refer to as marginally compliant. I was the type of student who half follows a teacher's instruction. I was the type of student who would never do enough to seriously get in trouble, but just enough to not be seen as a teacher's pet. I laughed when I heard a funny joke, participated in impromptu sports debates during class, but if asked to correct my behavior, I rarely put up a fight. Along those same lines, I would also consider myself a cusper. A cusper is a child who is academically middle of the pact. Their academic and social performance could go either way, depending on their life challenges. It also heavily depends on the support the child has in place to combat those challenges. When I first entered high school, this was the worst type of student to be. Why? Because most teachers simply overlooked you. I do not believe this was something teachers did intentionally. But, if you were not hot enough to make water boil or cold enough to make it freeze, you were left alone. I was practically invisible.

Sadly, the life I was beginning to live outside of school

was a different story. I found myself getting into a lot of trouble in the neighborhood where I grew up and, just years earlier, played as an innocent child. Several of my friends and I even started our own gang. Until later on in life, my mother would not believe some of the things I was involved in. She would occasionally receive a report or two from some of the neighbors in the area, but my mother never truly understood the acuteness of the situation. My mother always looked at me as the "good" child. Normally, my older brother and sister got into all of the trouble. When I started getting involved, she wasn't as keen on my behaviors. We had also moved to the other side of town, and most of the trouble I involved myself in was over by my grandparents' place.

My brother, Curtis, who began to see the changes in me, tried on multiple occasions to warn my mother of my actions and the things he knew I was getting involved in around the city. She would never believe him. Little did I know, I was in a very dangerous space in my life. The decisions I made over the next four years could determine my life's trajectory. By the midway point of freshman year, my trajectory was low. I had not involved myself in any extracurricular activities; I had a subpar grade point average and had an extreme lack of discipline. I was on my way to becoming invisible as I wasn't performing or vocalizing what I needed to be successful. I was definitely in a lose-lose situation and did not have a clue.

Growing up in the inner city of Cleveland, OH, education was not on the minds of most young people or their families. For most of us, our lives were less about preparing for our futures and more about learning how to navigate in an area where most only think of survival. Many of my friends, like myself, grew up impoverished. Our parents worked countless hours to only bring home $20,000 a year to support a family of four to five people. My mother, not having a college education herself, never really pushed me to go to college. Although my mother and other family members were loving and supportive, I do not recall having too many serious conversations about my future. Not saying the conversations never happened, just that none of them made me want to change my lifestyle. My mother had high expectations for me. I just did not live in a "going to college is the only option" type of household. Most of the conversations I recall having with my mom were about working hard, putting your best foot forward, and always being respectable. I do not remember ever having directed conversations about what I wanted to do, what college I wanted to attend, or where I saw myself within the next five to ten years.

As a result, I had no intention of going to college. Going into the second quarter of my freshman year, my academic performance was once again subpar as I carried around a 1.75 grade point average. I found myself spiraling down a path of self-destruction. I was poor, literally and figuratively. I had a lackluster attitude and lacked vision, as I could not see beyond my current circumstance. I once again found myself not believing in my abilities, but this time, it was academically. For most of my life, I had sat in classrooms unengaged, unfocused, and unmotivated. My uncle, who served as a constant source of motivation, had relocated due to advancement in his career. There was no consistent reaffirmation of success. Everyone simply lived their daily lives. People got up, went to work, paid bills when they could, and that was about it. If fortunate enough, we would take the occasional family vacation. However, those were few and far between. Like anything else in nature, I began to adapt to the environment surrounding me. I lacked positive male influences in my life. Although my mother did her best job to raise me, I did not have the proper guidance I needed to move into the next chapter of my life as a young man.

PART THREE

MENTORING MATTERS

D uring the 2007-08 school year, former Ohio Governor Ted Strickland made a promise to close the achievement gap in over thirty Ohio Schools. The gap? Studies showed that African American males who had failed two or more 8th grade classes, missed 30+ days of school, or were suspended for more than a week would more than likely drop out of school and not graduate. Unbeknownst to me, I was a young man who fit into this category due to my inadequate academic performance the year prior. To change this trajectory, Governor Strickland and former State Senator CJ Prentiss provided 20 million dollars in government funding over two years to offer mentorship and exposure opportunities to young men entering the 9th grade across the state of Ohio.

The Governor's Initiative to Close The Achievement Gap Program placed a linkage coordinator in high schools across the state to work specifically with incoming freshman male students. A linkage coordinator's job was to encourage young men to stay in school, keep track of our academic progression, expose us to different lifestyle options, and by "hook or crook," get us on the path to college. A linkage coordinator could be viewed as many things - a brother, counselor, therapist, mentor, friend, and for some, even a father. My linkage coordinator, Mr. George Golden, served as all of the above for me. He was my very first mentor and introduced me to a life I never knew existed. Although what he did for me was a part of his job, he went above and beyond the call of duty. He treated me like family — like his son.

Mr. Golden was the first person outside of my immediate family to take a genuine interest in my education. Mr. Golden took me on my first college tour and trip to the museum. He scorned me about my grades when I underperformed and was there when I experienced my first pregnancy scare as a senior in high school. At my high school graduation, he placed a stole around my neck, hugged me, and told me how proud he was of me and what I had accomplished.

With all transparency, I latched on to Mr. Golden so hard, I did not give him much of a choice. Almost 15 years later, I'm still not giving him much of a choice. I consistently call to check in with him or pick his brain for knowledge I do not possess. To this very day, I affectionately call him Dad. Mr. Golden entered my life during a time where I lacked focus and direction. Without his guidance, love, and leadership, I would not be the man I am today.

Mr. Golden (or Mr. G as many of the other students called him) and I crossed paths right before the midway point of my freshman year of high school. Mr. G was a very laid back but no-nonsense type of guy. He was a practical man who did not care much for excuses. He was solutions-oriented and hated complaining. If something was wrong, come up with a solution and fix it. If you did not like something, come up with a plan to change it. If you cannot change it, make the situation benefit you best as possible. Mr. G was a realist, and if you did not want to hear the truth, he wasn't the person to talk to. He would tell it like it was — no if's, and's, or but's about it.

Mr. G hosted workshops at the high school for young men in the freshman class. When I first started attending the workshops, I would only go because Mr. G would lure us into the conference room with pizza and wings. The only way to get the free food was to attend the full workshop, and I for sure wasn't missing out on an opportunity for free food. As I mentioned, the goal was getting us on the path to college, whether by hook or by crook. This was one of the prime examples.

The workshops covered a wide array of topics like college readiness, resume building, goal setting, summer employment opportunities, and proper table etiquette. I had no clue how much those workshops would shape my life and make me a more well-rounded person. Although I had not yet completely bought into The Closing the Achievement Gap Program or Mr. Golden, the program began to provide me a voice within my school community amongst my peers. The free pizza came as a bonus.

One of the most significant workshops for me came during the last semester of my freshman year. The workshop did not have a name, and Mr. Golden did not provide much insight about it. There was just a sign on the door that read, "Guest Speaker: Workshop begins at 4 PM. If you are late, do not enter." I remember inquiring about what would be taking place, and Mr. G's response was, "Cedric, you will find out what is happening when it is happening. Now go take a seat." This was such a typical Mr. Golden response. Luckily, I was smart enough to listen because this experience would soon alter my life.

The school day typically ended around 3 PM, and the workshops would start between 3:30 to 4 PM. On this particular day, the workshop did not start on time. Being the outspoken person I am, I began to do what Mr. Golden hated the most, complain. I insisted Mr. G give us the Church's Chicken that had been ordered for the day's program for our inconvenience. Of course, Mr. G declined and made me take my seat and stop my protest as I was getting the other students stirred up. Around 4:10 PM, our guest speaker walked into the conference room. He was a young brother; he looked to be no more than 25 years old. He wore a distressed pair of denim jeans, a pair of all-black Chuck Taylors, a blazer, neck scarf, and a Kangol hat. My first immediate thought was, "Who is this clown?" I had never seen anyone dressed like this before. At least not where I was from. We continued to chatter amongst ourselves as he walked over to Mr. Golden and shook his hand. After their brief salutation, Mr. Golden immediately brought order to the room.

At the beginning of each workshop, Mr. G would lay down the ground rules. It would be the typical things you would say to a group of immature 9th-grade boys who lacked self-control and discipline. "Listen up. This gentleman is here to provide you with some insight that could be beneficial to your lives. Focus up, pay attention, and be respectful. If you cannot handle those simple directions, leave now. We do not have time for foolishness." As you could imagine, after that message, we all calmed down, took our seats, and focused on the speaker, who, at the time, none of us were impressed with. He was simply the one thing standing between the Church's Chicken in the corner of the room and us.

The speaker began to introduce himself. "What's going on, gentlemen? I hope all is well, and you're in good spirits. My name is Basheer Jones, and I'm happy to be able to share this space with you today to talk about..."

To this very day, I still do not know what came over me and possessed me to do so, but I interjected and said, "You're late." The whole room looked stunned, Basheer and Mr. Golden included. Basheer began to laugh, and a brief dialogue between the two of us ensued.

BASHEER: So I'm late, huh?

ME: Yes, you're late.

BASHEER: Oh, okay. So what time was I supposed to be here?

ME: You were supposed to be here at 4 o'clock. It's 4:17.

BASHEER: Nah, I was supposed to be here at 4:30.

ME: It says it on the door, "Workshop starts at 4:00 PM."

(Basheer turned to look at the door.)

BASHEER: It does say that, huh? Aight, little brother. You're right. I tell you what. I'm going to be spending the next five weeks with you all. If I am ever late again, I am going to make you responsible for holding me accountable. Deal?

ME: Deal!

BASHEER: But just know, I'm also going to hold you accountable too.

ME: Hold me accountable for what? You were the one who was late.

(The other boys began to laugh.)

BASHEER: I'm going to hold you accountable for being your best self. I talk to Mr. Golden often, and I'm going to check on you. Deal?

(The boys responded with oohs.)

I was a little more reluctant to accept this deal than the first one. I felt like I had bit off more than I could chew, and I would have a target on my back. Basheer persisted again. "So, do we have a deal?"

I responded, "Yes." From there, the iron sharpens iron framework was put into place.

After regaining control of the room, Basheer continued to introduce himself. He was a Clevelander and a product of Cleveland Public Schools from the Martin Luther King High, Jr. High School campus. He also introduced himself as a Morehouse Man, who was the youngest radio talk show host in the country at that time. He informed us that we would be focusing on the power of words and the impact they have on our everyday lives over the next several weeks.

None of this mattered to me at the time. I was more impressed with how confidently he spoke. He was young but very wise for his age. You could feel his passion fill the room as he stood in front of us. As a young successful black man, you could tell he wanted more for his life and ours.

He captured the room and came off as insightful, powerful, and unapologetically black. Quite frankly, I had never heard anyone talk like him before. He was polished and modest while all in the same breath, bold and fearless.

The first workshop started with Basheer asking us what type of music we listened to, when we listened to the music, and how often. He told us the things we regularly listened to would ultimately shape who we were as people. Why? Basheer's theory was that when you repeatedly do something or listen to something, your mind begins to internalize the ideas. He would say, "What we internalize is what we will manifest." He went on to say that most of the music we consumed daily was more negative than positive. He spoke about how the lyrics in some of the songs tricked our young black men and women into being portrayed as thugs or sex objects. He spoke the truth but as an ally, not as someone trying to tear down the culture.

I was hooked; not only was he engaging, so was the topic. I loved to rap and loved listening to rap music. This workshop was right up my alley, and thanks to my antics at the beginning of the session, he expected me to answer questions. I guess I deserved it, and I did not shy away from the challenge. I provided the most articulate answers I possibly could. For the first time in several school years, I found myself trying to sound and be intelligent. Although he did not say it, I could tell he and I had gained one another's respect. By the end of the first session, I was no longer interested in just the food. I was more interested in getting to know Basheer and his journey.

After the workshop was over, Basheer stayed around and

hung out with us for a while. He even enjoyed some of the chicken we all longed for. While we ate, we continued our conversation about music and who some of our favorite artists were. Then finally, the question came. "Do any of you rap?" Basheer asked. A few of us raised our hands, myself included. Basheer said, "Okay, let's do it," and he started going in with a freestyle. No beat on the table, no beatbox, just him, and he was spitting straight bars. Basheer's flow was different. He talked about black life but from the lenses of activists and cultural thought leaders like Malcolm X and Martin Luther King, Jr.. He spoke about W.E.B. DuBois and Frederick Douglas as the people he idolized and wanted to shape his life after. His message was positive, but not like Will Smith's positive rap. His style was more, like radical, black liberation positive, and he had a swagger that made it sound appealing.

After Basheer finished rapping his verse, we all roared with applause and cheered. He was good — really good. He was easily one of the best I had ever heard. You could hear the other students' chatter about how good he was and how impressed they were by his raps. If he hadn't gotten our attention throughout the workshop, he was receiving it now. As others applauded, Basheer waited for the next person to spit their verse in the cypher. All of the other students shied away after hearing him rap and felt too embarrassed. They did not feel they had the skill to keep up. So, I jumped in:

"Ayo Nute, (Nute was my big homie from the neighborhood I grew up in) tell'em to come stop me
Only way you keep me from moving is if you pop me

Yes, I like to bounce in the ring like I was Rocky
You can smell what I cook in the kitchen just like the Rock be
Stay hard
All the time just like a rock be
Throw my hands up in a diamond
This ain't no rock beat
Because my hood made a dynasty
Perfect example from a prince to a king
Just come and watch me
See the bright light on my wrist?
That's where my watch be
Yeah, you see how bright it is do not ask me what time it is
Crazy flow
Hip is where the llama is
Bad thing to say I'm always where the drama is
Always where the paper is
Call me the chasing kid
Play with mine, and imma toss'em five like I was Jason Kidd
All Nets all the time just like Jason Kidd
Snap back, crack ya neck, then I'm gonna break ya ribs
Call the cops
Because the way I came, I'm breaking in
Two face shots man
That means that I'm breaking chins
The whips clumsy
My screen fell down again
Came threw swervin
Man, they think I'm drunk
Pop trunk, Swang doors
Bring the bases in

Alfonso Soreona, man, the way I run the bases in
Money Money only thing that I'm chasing, man
Keep a couple stacks in my hand
I got a couple grand
27 Inch Titans call me Eddie George
I'm throwed sitting sideways while I'm swinging doors
And we keep the system bumping, man, we making noise
When it come to the trunk game, I got the latest toys
Know what I'm claiming, man, I'm messing with them Glenville boys
Got no choice but to feel us
We untamed gorillas
My boys greedy, man, scraping the plate
Hungry in these streets dog, but we already ate"

As I finished, the other boys went wild with cheers and applause. Basheer was impressed too. He shook my hand and nodded his head in agreement with the others. The energy from the crowd gave me a rush, and once again, I felt great about myself. Although everything else in my life was of subpar caliber, my rapping was the one thing that made me feel elite. The words I recited in my verses gave me a voice. Rapping gave me a chance to be seen, heard, and respected by my peers. It was the one thing in my life I was extremely proud of. It was the only thing in my life I consistently put effort into.

Once a week for the next five weeks, Basheer would come to my school and host more workshops. As the workshops went on, the exercises became more intense and focused on words — how important they are to our futures and how we use them. We talked about the impact of the music we listened to, the impact of our conversations with others, and ultimately, how we speak to ourselves. Basheer's goal was to teach us that words were powerful and that the words or thoughts we internalized (consciously or subconsciously) would manifest in our everyday lives.

Basheer commonly used analogies about food and a balanced diet to drive his points home. He'd say things like, "If you consistently consume unhealthy foods, you will become unhealthy. There is no way around it. No matter how much you exercise, you will lack energy and focus. You will begin to feel sluggish and unmotivated. I'm not saying you should not ever eat unhealthy food — because afterwards, we are going to eat that Church's Chicken. You have to do it in moderation. You have to have balance."

Basheer taught me being healthy should not just be a physical aspiration. He stressed that our mental, spiritual, and emotional health were just as important, if not more important, as being physically fit. Basheer ingrained in us that the most powerful things we could do as young black men were to control our emotions, be conscious, and think before acting or reacting to any situation. Basheer emphasized that we should never make life-altering decisions based on emotions — our every move should be calculated. On the contrary, he stripped away the idea that men expressing their emotions was a sign of weakness. He told us that as black men, it is okay to express our emotions, passions, and anger — as long as it's channeled correctly. He promoted listening to positive music, reading books, and consuming knowledge to enrich our spirits. Our sessions with Basheer were extremely informative and gave me a new outlook on life. I looked forward to each week as I became more positive and socially aware. Those workshops helped me grow and learn skills that would benefit my future. And, of course, at the end of every session, we rapped.

"Pass me the mic on this rhythm, shake
Beats I'll obliterate
Never slowing down because I always accelerate
Do not stop running just because you'll lose the race
But in this race, you'll lose so please come participate
Trash guys like garbage men
The garbage is them
I'm undefeated and that statement needs no repeating
And boys who wanna test me
Get popped like Pepsi
My flow is like an illness
They call me epilepsy
They do not say I'm fresh for no reason
I raise blood pressures
Call me diabetes
Flows come easy like rhymes from the heavens
Sixteen bars, more verses than your Reverend
Feel the heat like radiation
I know that I'm hot
Spit a verse to my roof and converted the top
Quit talking
Flows hit hard like Brian Dawkins
Chicken squawking while I'm walking but no time for questions
I mustn't

I have to push it hard like a point guard
And my flow is strong like my deodorant, Right Guard
And I'm a legend in this game just call me Brett Farve
You cats need to roll and bounce like a basketball
Steve Young with the flow, how I'm passing y'all
Talking all that homicide I'll give you what you're asking for
Crush sucka boy
Flow polished like Armor All
Cannot be touched just like I had some armor on
Straightened out just like I had the iron on
I'm the flyest rapper in the game I would not lie to y'all
Trust the boy
I'm not average I'm extraordinary
That means everything I do is out the ordinary
And your flows are like dead weight out the cemetery
They tell me, "Cedric, go to hell!"
I say, "I been already!"
I'm bout my chips and cheese call me nachos
Hot flows, I can raise the roof or I can break the floor
It depends on whichever the spot goes
I blow on you flimsy toilet paper flow call me snot-nose"

Our final session was a bit different from the rest. We watched a film, so our session was shorter, with less lecturing from Basheer. The film featured some ideas of black excellence and some words from Tupac Shakur. After the video, Basheer ended the session by saying, "We can all be roses in the concrete. Before I go, I am going to leave you with a poem."

Now I have heard Basheer rap, and he was also a great

speaker, but a poem? Although I appreciated poetry, I never thought of it as being parallel to rap. Poetry, in my mind, was mainly soft and sappy. Also, my immature mind believed that poetry was just for girls. I had not yet been introduced to the likes of James Baldwin, Amari Baraka, or Paul Laurence Dunbar. To that end, the boys in my neighborhood did not write poetry. We rapped, and typically, we all rapped about the same things. So when I heard poetry coming from Basheer, I was shocked.

Basheer began to recite his piece confidently and composed as he had always been. He had the poem memorized from top to bottom. It came off to me as more than just poetry, but I could not describe it. It was something I could hear and feel at the same time. His words came alive and jumped out at us as we sat in our seats. This was my first introduction to spoken word, and this moment would inspire and change me. His words were not just for the page; he delivered them with vigor and conviction. Afterward, he told us that spoken word was meant to be heard and to evoke emotions in those who were listening. With his words, Basheer created a visible grotesque image of America that was hard to erase from memory. He was good.

After Basheer finished his piece, he stayed for a few more moments to bid us all a farewell, sensing this would be our last session with him. He assured us that although this was his last session with us, it would not be his last time with us. He encouraged us to stay positive, consume positive things, and listen to more positive music. He encouraged us not to give in to the world and its social constructs of black men. He assured us we were free to be whoever and whatever we wanted to be. The most significant thing to come out of our last session was Basheer's mandate for me. He challenged me to keep writing and building my brand as an artist. However, he charged me to write more positively. As I participated in his workshops, I began to realize how negative my raps and thoughts were. An overwhelming majority of them talked about violence, greed, sexism, and murder. The majority of my raps had an overwhelming amount of cursing in them too. Basheer challenged me to use my gift (as he would call it) to uplift those in my community — not tear them down. More specifically, he challenged me to write a spoken word piece others could look to for inspiration. He mandated me to be a positive force in my community and change for the better.

"We all have a light, a gift that the creator has blessed us with. Each one of them is unique and specific to you. It is up to you how you use your gift. Will you use your gift for evil? Or, will you use it to uplift those around you?" Basheer told us. "And, young brother, I'm going to be expecting that poem," he said to me as he gave us a soft bow and departed.

For the next couple of days, I wrestled with Basheer's challenge. I had never written a poem or any significantly positive rap. I was at a standstill and did not have many ideas to draw from. Since I did not have a knowledge base from which to formulate words that would inspire others, I started reading.

I began to research some of the people Basheer spoke about in his sessions. I was amazed at all of the information I garnered. From a Google search, I was introduced to a whole new world. One link led to another link, and one person connected me to another. Over 100 black influential people went across my computer screen. I became obsessed with learning about these people and their stories. These black faces began to tell me a story of a different America, one that could only be understood by the constituents of the generational curse of systemic racism.

During my research, I found a whole world of black literature I never knew existed. I found black authors, poets, and intellectuals! This wasn't necessarily the first time I had heard of black excellence. In school, we had the typical conversations about the same select few African American leaders from the Civil Rights and Black Power Movements of the '50s, '60s, and '70s. But it was nothing like this. There were so many names, faces, and people with stories untold — untapped. For me, it was an extraordinary but unusual feeling. Why had I never heard of these people before? I wondered. Obviously, other people knew who they were. Every year, we were reintroduced to the same people repeatedly, but there were so many more stories to tell. I began to feel like people were hiding this information from me as if this was information someone did not want me to know.

Their stories were tales of triumph, but these black faces told the story of "The Other America," where everyone is not treated equally, and blacks are seen as inferior humans. My research made me realize how wonderfully complex, beautiful, conflicted, powerful, yet vulnerable black people were. It gave me a new perspective on life. For the first time in my life, at 13 years old, I consciously accepted that I was a black man in America. More importantly, I accepted that being black in America would cause me problems, and being a conscious black man would cause me even more.

For the next several weeks, I read the books and articles of black thought leaders from across several decades. I read about Frederick Douglas, W.E.B. DuBois, Marcus Garvey, Stockley Carmichael, and the Black Panther Party, Booker T. Washington, Henry Highland Garnet, William Wells Brown, Langston Hughes, Sojourner Truth, and many more. As I read their accomplishments, I grew proud of my people. I became proud of our lineage and where we came from as African Americans.

In addition to feeling empowered, I also grew infuriated as I read more and explored the plight of African Americans. I questioned how people who had contributed so much to society could be treated as second class citizens, less than human, and chattel. Although I was enthralled with all of the accomplishments of my people, I was disgusted with the idea of a country selling false tales of life, liberty, and the pursuit of happiness. Although I would not be able to fully understand the pedagogy of knowledge I consumed until later during my studies at Morehouse, I grappled with Ralph Ellison's idea of being invisible, with James Baldwin's assertion that conscious blacks in America live in a constant state of rage, and Du Bois' declaration of the color-line and living behind a black veil. Through their writings, I found struggle. I found hardship. I found homelessness. I found despair. I found agony. I found apathy. I found depression. I found hunger. I found hopelessness. I found agitation. I found misunderstanding. I found confusion. From reading their works, I found a multitude of facets depicting black life in America. In the fullness of time, I found myself. I could relate to many of the experiences I read. For the first time in a while, I connected to what I read. These were the first writers that struck me outside of the writers of The BoxCar Children series I read in the third grade.

For the first time, I truly understood that equal rights and protection under the law wasn't meant for people of a darker hue. I understood the promises made to all American citizens were not truly meant for the likes of blacks. No matter how hard black people tried, we would always be met with systemic opposition.

Everything Basheer had said to us during the workshops, everything Mr. Golden expressed about getting a quality education, and everything my mother told me about being respectful, putting my best foot forward, and working hard finally made sense. They were not telling me things I should do to be a better person. They were telling me what I needed to do in order to survive in a world designed for me to fail.

After digesting all the pain, suffering, and anguish my people had endured and continued to endure, I wept. My tears led me to completing the spoken word piece Basheer challenged me to write. It only took me twenty minutes. The words poured right out of me. When I finished, I was exhausted like I had worked a full day of intense labor in a Mississippi cotton field. My body was drained, and all I could remember was waking up the next day to get ready for school. When I opened my eyes, my notebook was adjacent to my head. I flipped to what I had written the night before and began to recite the poem to myself.

Our Life, Our History

Black History, Black History
Is what I live every day because of the complexion of my skin
Dark blast from the past make my future so dim
Being stereotyped makes my personality grim
Back in Virginia in 1619 is where slavery began
Being stripped of their dignity and moved away from the motherland
The United States of America is where their new life begins
1787 is when slavery becomes legal
Just to physically and mentally destroy my people
Jim Crow laws of the south made sure there were no equals
So families had to suffer because of their black color
Did not even care about children and black mothers
Men of the law abusing our black brothers
And the great grandmothers who have to scrape for supper
These are the people who are the backbone of our struggle
399 men left to die in Tuskegee
Hosed down by policeman that started riots in Montgomery
What I'm saying is no illusion
All is real
Equal rights for all men?
Tell that to Emmitt Till
Tell that to the innocent man who cannot post bail
They even made Eddie Murphy spend life in a cell
Brown vs. Board of Education made it to the Supreme Court
Emancipation Proclamation was supposed to free us
Makes me think that we shouldn't be celebrating July 4th
Malcolm X assassinated while giving a speech in New York
I do not know if it's me personally or my race that you want to

destroy
You cannot take me away from my history
No way to change how many people died
They tried to kill us all and create their own version of genocide
Captured and seized
Brought on a boat across seas
Filled with disease
Packed so tight that they could not even breathe
Shackled down and chained up
My people abused and bent up
Willie used to lynch us
But you cannot tell me my people did not make a difference
Men who were called mules were forced to do incest
Battered and bruised and hung to burn like incense
No respect if you were black
No matter adult, toddler, or infant
We did not ask to be in this nation
You brought us into the position
Brought Africans here to build
But now we're the oppositions
Hypersexualize, Criminalize, and ship us off to prison
Every day I wake up and pray that somehow life could be different
I'm at a loss with it all
Someone make it make sense
I'm listening

The words were so piercing that they did not seem as if they were my own. The frustration, anger, and passion written in the poem made some very significant changes in me. That morning, as I stood in the bathroom mirror and brushed my teeth, I made a commitment to myself to be a better person, learn more about my people, and ultimately do what I knew was right. I began to focus my energy on more constructive activities and became slightly more secluded. All I wanted to do was read black literature. I obsessed over it almost just as much as I obsessed over writing. My trust in the world around me had been jaded. I looked at everyone, black and white, in a different light. Those novels, stories, anthologies, and poems were the only things that brought me comfort and understanding of the world around me. One of my teachers inquired why all the material I read was "so serious". Time and time again, she insisted I read other types of books, but I refused. I wanted to make my ancestors proud by proving wrong those who thought we were nothing. I did not know everything I needed to do to accomplish my goal, but I was determined to give it my best shot.

I am sincerely thankful to Basheer for leading those workshops at my school. I thank him for shining light on our people's true history and leaving me curious enough to read more on my own. I admired his leadership and boldness at such a young age. I appreciate Basheer for igniting a flame in me to be a better person, live a life of consequence, and know the history from which I truly originated. I love him dearly for the challenge he presented me and for sharpening my iron. Challenging me to write the inspirational poem and promoting a more positive message required me to think more critically about what I was saying. Since that time, all of my raps or poems have had an uplifting message. Without Basheer, I would not be the poet I am today. Thanks to Basheer, my words were infused with a true purpose — to change the perception of those in my community.

Mr. Golden continued to host workshops and enrichment sessions at Glenville. When the weather got warmer, we went on college tours and took trips to museums and local theatres. We even took long road trips out of the city. Our first long road trip came during spring break of my freshman year. We went to Charleston, South Carolina to learn about the city's history through visiting museums, memorial sites, and slave plantations. We learned of the Gullah Geechee culture in South Carolina and how tumultuous it was to work on a paddy field's swampy terrain. We even took an African rhythm class where they taught us drums and dances from West Africa. Charleston was rich with African American Culture. Some of the first slaves were brought there to toil her lands. Although the culture and history of South Carolina were deeply rooted in slavery, it still struck me as a beautiful place with its cobblestone streets lined with palm trees. The Atlantic Ocean ran elegantly adjacent to the city. I told Mr. Golden that I loved Charleston so much, I would one day retire there. Looking back, this was a profound statement in my life. This statement was probably the first outward projection I ever made about my future — a long term goal. It is a goal I still aspire to achieve to this day.

All of these opportunities and experiences began to alter my life for the better. I still wasn't a straight-A-student, but I began to focus more on my work. The report cards that were usually full of C's now had a few B's and A's sprinkled in between. I attended Mr. Golden's workshops regularly and followed through on any assignments he gave me to complete outside of my necessary school work. The work I put in was being noticed, and although I wasn't as consistent as I should have been, I was trying my best to create new habits in my life.

A few weeks after returning to school from spring break, I was presented with an opportunity. This day forever remains freshly minted in mind as one of the most important days of my young adult life. One afternoon, I was in my world history class, and Mr. Golden appeared at the door. He gave the door a slight knock and entered. All of the students' attention was now on him. He waited until the teacher acknowledged him and then asked if he could borrow me for a few moments. The teacher obliged, and Mr. Golden gestured for me to follow him into the hallway. After closing the classroom door behind me, he asked if I would be open to an opportunity to travel by plane to Atlanta, GA. He informed me that the trip would be centered around the 2008 Morehouse College Commencement Ceremony. Oddly enough, I did not even know what a commencement was. I had never heard the word.

The only deterring factor was that this trip was not with Mr. Golden or my school. It was with another linkage coordinator from Martin Luther King, Jr. High School. I only knew one other person from MLK, my longtime friend, EJ, so I would be on my own. I told Mr. Golden I was down for the trip but would have to discuss it with my mother. Mr. Golden assured me everything would be fine. He knew the other linkage coordinator and trusted him. He even promised me the opportunity to meet the MLK linkage coordinator before the trip.

Although a little shocked, I was more than excited to be

selected for the trip. To this day, I do not understand why I was picked, the criteria for selection, or the conversations that led to my selection, but I am so happy it was me. The rest of the school day felt like an eternity. I was eager to get home and talk to my mom. As soon as school was over, I ran to the bus stop and headed home. After school, I typically stopped by my grandparents' house to eat all of their food and hang out with my friends in the neighborhood, but not that day. I aimed straight for home.

After a long day at work, my mother would come home, get comfortable, and disappear into her room to rest. I was determined to catch her before she rested. I met her at the door and started rambling. At this point, my mother had met Mr. Golden because many of the program's out of town excursions required parents to attend an informational. Since she was familiar with him and the program's benefits, I did not anticipate a hard time convincing her to permit me to go.

My mother genuinely wanted me to attend the trip, but she could not afford accommodations for a plane ticket and hotel room on such short notice. In a matter of seconds, my dreams of flying to Atlanta were crushed, and I went to my room feeling defeated. The next day, I informed Mr. Golden that I would not be able to travel to Atlanta due to my financial situation at home. Mr. Golden chuckled as I told him. Initially, I was slightly offended that he would laugh at my sorrow and misfortune. He then explained that the trip was free of charge; the governor and the program I was now an active member of would provide the funds. I walked with Mr. Golden to his office and called my mother immediately to see if the waived fees would change her mind. Mr. Golden spoke with my mother, provided her more information about the trip, and informed her that I could attend at no expense to her. My mother agreed to let me go, and Mr. Golden and I were ecstatic. After we ended the call with my mother, Mr. Golden provided me with all the information to secure my place on the trip. I had to attend an orientation at Martin Luther King High School with a parent. At the orientation, we would meet the linkage coordinator and the man responsible for coordinating this life-altering trip to Atlanta, Mr. Timothy Roberts, Sr.

Over the next few weeks, I began to inquire about Mr. Roberts. As I began to ask teachers and others in the school community, I found that he was very well known and popular. Most people had a lot of great things to say about the work he had done with the youth in the community. He was described as a tall brown-skinned man who stood about 6'5 and weighed 230 pounds with a raspy voice. He was a former police officer for the city and security guard at MLK prior to becoming the linkage coordinator. He was also the basketball coach of the Junior Varsity team at my high school. This was news to me, as I had never seen him before. All things considered, I felt more comfortable with meeting Mr. Roberts after the completion of my analysis.

I was beyond anxious as I entered MLK Jr. High School for orientation. I was thankful for my mother's presence and support because I needed it. When my mother and I walked into the cafeteria, several families were seated and waiting as others conversed and congregated around the perimeter of the room. There were also two filming crews. One of them was a popular local news station in Cleveland. A very tall man with a raspy voice stood at the front of the room and greeted everyone who came in. Based on the description and other information I gathered, I knew this gentleman was indeed Mr. Roberts. After my mother and I found a table, I helped myself to the refreshments in the back of the room.

Mr. Roberts called for everyone's attention, and the orientation began. Mr. Roberts was a very well-spoken and well-dressed man. He was excited about the opportunity to lead young people on such a legendary trip, and you could hear it in his voice. After a few moments of listening to Mr. Roberts speak, I could tell he was a true dreamer. He was a visionary, full of grand ideas waiting to be executed. With wisdom and confidence, he shared his heart on the plight of young black men in the city of Cleveland and how this trip could potentially change the narrative. Emotion would often fill his eyes as he expressed the significance of this trip. I was instantly drawn to Mr. Roberts, his style, mannerisms, and candidness. He instantly became a larger than life figure in my eyes, and I knew Mr. Golden had sent me to the correct place.

During our orientation, Mr. Roberts also discussed our trip's itinerary, the excursions we would take along the way, our flight, and all of the other details of our trip. Just hearing the trip's details got me excited, and to put the icing on the cake, all of the young men attending the trip to Morehouse would receive a brand new free tailored suit - including a belt, shoes, and a tie. After he gave his spill, Mr. Roberts introduced the other individuals who would play a part in the trip. Each of them shared how special our trip to the historic

Morehouse would be. I did not know much about Morehouse or its history, but I was thrilled about visiting Atlanta.

I could tell our final speaker was sort of a big deal because Mr. Roberts gave a grand introduction for him. Mr. Roberts described the speaker as an MLK Jr. High School Graduate, Morehouse Alum, poet, radio talk show host, and community activist. It sounded like someone I knew, but I wasn't too sure. Mr. Roberts shared the work he had done with this individual and how proud he was of him. Mr. Roberts finished his heartfelt introduction, "Without any further ado, I introduce to some and reintroduce to others, my son, Basheer Jones.

I was ecstatic! The room erupted for Basheer as if he was everyone's son. He walked to the front of the room with urgency and confidence and shared with us Morehouse's significance to the world. That day I learned that Morehouse College was the only college in the country designed specifically to educate African American men. Basheer told us of some notable Morehouse alumni and how it was one of the most esteemed institutions in the country. In my fervent study of black excellence, I'd never read anything about Morehouse. However, I did learn about the great people who attended, like Martin Luther King Jr., Samuel L. Jackson, and Spike Lee. I could not wait to grace Morehouse's grounds like so many greats before me had done. That evening, my mother and I left the orientation feeling inspired and hopeful. Not only did I have the opportunity to go on a trip of a lifetime for free, but I also gained a new mentor in the process.

Over the years, my student-mentor relationship with Mr.

Roberts evolved into a father-son relationship. I affectionately call him Pops and treat him as such. He affectionately calls me his son and has treated me in the same regard. He has continuously encouraged me and poured life into me. Without Mr. Roberts, I would not be a Morehouse Man or a proud member of Alpha Phi Alpha Fraternity, Inc., of which all of his "sons" are now apart.

At this juncture, I want to thank all of the men mentioned in this chapter for their unrelenting efforts to encourage and inspire the next generation of young people. Your continued growth over the past fifteen years has encouraged me to continue to strive for greatness. I also want to express my gratitude to the families that shared these men with me. In situations such as these, it is not always easy to be selfless, to share something that ultimately belongs to you. Thank you all for sharing your fathers and husbands with me as mine was absent. These men have made the world a better place for myself and many others. To the Golden, Jones, and Roberts families, thank you!

To Dad and Pop, thank you for allowing me in your homes, to sit at your tables, and to eat your food. Thank you for allowing me to be around your children and serve as a positive influence for them. Thank you for nurturing me during a time when I needed it the most. For a long time, I did not have a father figure. Now, I brag every Father's Day because I have two. I am extremely blessed to have you both.

PART FOUR

FROM CLEVELAND TO MOREHOUSE

The day before the trip, all attendees slept overnight at the local community center to ensure no one was left behind, and everyone was ready for our trip to Atlanta. We had an early morning flight, and Mr. Roberts did not leave anything to chance. He wanted to confirm everyone selected to go on the trip would be there. He knew that this trip would be an experience of a lifetime for many of us.

When we entered the community center, Mr. Roberts greeted us at the door with a checklist of all of the things he required students to bring on the trip. He checked for toiletries, adequate clothing, and of course, the pristine suit and all of its accessories: khaki dress pants, black blazer, white collared shirt, black belt, black shoes, and most symbolic, the black and old gold necktie and handkerchief. He checked off each name until all 24 students were present and accounted for at the community center. Several chaperones, as well as a cameraman, were also traveling with us. There were about 31 people in total. We ate dinner together and talked about the trip and the experience we hoped to have. We all went to sleep eager and filled with excitement for what the next day had to offer.

At 4:15 AM, Mr. Roberts was rumbling around waking students. I honestly do not think he slept at all. I was already half-awake as I could not find comfort on the hard floor. Although I appreciated the community center for allowing us to rest there free of charge, the accommodations were far from plush. Each young man took turns going into the restroom, washing his face, and brushing his teeth. Mr. Roberts sounded off like an alarm in the background, generating urgency. I recall him consistently clapping his hands, saying, "It is showtime, gentlemen!" He exuded enthusiasm as if he had just won a 12 round heavyweight title bout. Little did we know, we would be the victors.

By 5:30 AM, we were all dressed and boarding a charter bus that would take us to Cleveland Hopkins International Airport on the city's westside. For many of us, it was our first time going to an airport. It was not a regular experience for many kids living in the inner city of Cleveland. So, I had to live out this opportunity to the fullest. We arrived at the airport, luggage in hand, ready to take on the world. Then, fear started to settle in. We would be flying at top speed thousands of miles above the ground with only air and cement to break our fall. This would be my first flight, and I could feel the anxiety getting the best of me.

As we received our flight itinerary from the ticketing agent, many of us began to protest taking the flight. Maybe it was the fear of flying. Perhaps it was the fear of dying, mid-air. Or, maybe it was being exposed to something new that frightened us the most. Luckily, courageous we stood, and none of us turned back. Our chaperones would not allow us to anyway. They would consistently say things like, "We made it this far, and we do not take any backward steps." as motivation and encouragement.

The walk through the airport was extremely peculiar. I felt like a celebrity, a superstar, but only for a moment. People were in awe at such a large group of teenage black boys at the airport at one time. They inquired about who we were, what we were doing, and where we were headed. Most assumed we were a high school sports team of some sort. We were consistently asked if we played football or basketball. Although we all loved sports, we took pride in letting them know we were not an athletics team; we were a group of young men going to experience the college graduation of black men who looked just like us. We told them we were going to Morehouse College. While some applauded this action, many people became disinterested and no longer wanted to talk. Some did not even wish us well on our flight.

For many years, I reflected upon those encounters at the airport and wrestled with my feelings. Until my sophomore year at Morehouse, I held a grudge against those strangers because of their inaccurate perceptions. An athlete! That is it? Nothing came to their minds except the stereotypical identification of a group of young black men going somewhere. These incidents made me reflect upon the conversation I had with Basheer during our workshops. It made me sick to know this was my reality and the reality of many others like me. It also brought more focus and insight to why Mr. Roberts and others felt a trip of this magnitude was so imperative.

As we approached the gate to board our plane, the trip gained a new meaning. It was no longer just an all-expense paid getaway. I wanted to prove the negative people in the airport wrong. I wanted to show them black boys could be athletes and more if we so dreamed. I wanted to learn everything about Morehouse and its legacy. I wanted to know why some people referred to Morehouse as a powerhouse school or a place where all black men should aspire to go for college. People even referred to Morehouse as a part of the "Black Ivy League." Although today, I would disdain any notion of my institution being the Black Ivy League, at the time, it sounded appealing. Morehouse is simply Morehouse, and that has always been good enough. I would use this trip to gather as much knowledge about the institution as possible. Ultimately, this trip would save me from a life I once knew as the only life I could live.

We boarded our plane, took our seats, and settled in for the ride. Though we were anxious, most of us fell asleep immediately after takeoff.

LOVE IN MY CITY

So I said, thank you to those who are giving back to the youth
As you sit and listen as this young brother speaks the truth
As I uncover what's true
You better not keep a dirty dinner because I'm everywhere
like 19 action news
So go and get my filming crew
And tell them to record the world as we see it
Make the blind see it,
the deaf hear it
 and the scared no longer fear it
 because in this race to be great
you have to be fierce
But this is more than just poetry
This is more than just delivery
This is dear to me
Because like deer to me, we are scared of the headlights
And everyone else will tell you it is because you are not bright
But you see, we are just shy
We do not like the positive attention and I do not know why
Maybe because the bad is the only thing they pay attention to

You get more praise for going to prison than for going to
Princeton and to this I just cry
You'll let one brother kill your brother
And then you get his name tattooed on your side
Teardrops under the left eye to represent the pain
We wear rags and bandanas just to represent a gang
And we die over the streets we claim
And this is insane
And it's pointless
It's like trying to breathe with no air
So let's sit back for a moment
Let's do it like a movie that's playing and your mother calls
your name to pause it
You're telling me we're willing to die over a street
When we do not own anything on it
The deaths are pointless
My community is sick and she needs a doctor's appointment
So, I guess I'll have to play pediatrician
All the signs of destruction are calling our names
Are you listening?
5% of the world's population
But 25% remain in prisons
And they're building even more
So many jails are being built that they will eventually be at
our front doors
They will not build us new schools but they'll build us prisons
worth millions
So you can tell me where their mental is
But that is because we fail
Dr. Martin Luther King Jr. Said

"Silence is the greatest betrayal"
And so far
We have been silent
But we make noise for the violence
Then scatter when we hear the sirens
We need change
No cliche of Obama and Joe Biden
So we must look to our Horizons
And then look back at our success
If we all played our parts
We could all mobilize the streets to lead us out of the dark
But I lived on the east side of East High
And they're still trying to bomb us
So I give praise to the Granville T. Woods and the Obamas
I give praise to the mothers
I give praise to the brothers…. And the sisters
I give praise to a cause that's much bigger
I get intoxicated off of the truth
Not liquor
I do it for the one who created the sun
For the man who gave his only begotten son
The one who we call number one
I do it for He
Because everything I have done
He has done triple from me
So When it comes to giving praise you hear no tripping from
me
It's nothing but a blessing you see
And life may get hectic
I'm just happy to be alive to deliver this message

He gave me the length to reach for it
The hands to grab it
The power to lift and a gift of speech that turns heads backward
And then there is laughter at the amazement
So It's all love to the Most High
We should all praise Him
But it's all about the birth and the death
And life is what you do in-between time
So in the meantime
Make your time mean something
Do not be an ignorant, arrogant, hater
Do not be the rigid, statistic, unstable
Be the loving, caring, joy that somebody needs
And if one does it
Then Twenty follow
Let's make this happiness spread like a disease
Let's make it stick to the scalp
Like Weave
Then we can all leave
Like Trees
To a place where we can always feel the Bahama breeze
And if nothing more
I'll be following the teachings of the greats until they throw me off the ocean shore
And when I'm buried six feet under the ocean floor
I will always follow the examples that were made
Because the proof is here
I'm just gonna end it on a line right here
The truth was here

PART FIVE

THE MOREHOUSE MYSTIQUE

When we arrived to Morehouse, I could feel something special in the air. To this day, I cannot tell you exactly what it was, but its presence was apparent. Maybe it was the freshly cut green luscious sea waving in the wind before me — each blade gently caressed by the warm summer breeze. Perhaps it was the eyes of the Rev. Dr. Martin Luther King, Jr. peering down on us from his perch in front of the international chapel bearing his name. Or, maybe it was the spirit of Dr. Benjamin Elijah Mays safeguarding the integrity of Century Campus, protecting its legacy from those who would try to cross its legendary ash-filled pastures in just a few days. The grounds were beautiful, and from the time I stepped foot on the campus, Morehouse felt like home.

After descending safely into Hartsfield Jackson International Airport, a charter bus picked us up from the airport's lower level and transported us to our hotel and then to the college. The charter bus would be our mode of transportation for the week. The bus had several TVs, a nice restroom, and adequate space for everyone to spread out and get comfortable. It was the most efficient and cost-effective way to move 24 youngsters around the city of Atlanta. Although we went to see the Morehouse College Commencement Ceremony, Mr. Roberts and the other coordinators planned a trip that allowed us to experience Atlanta as a whole. We also visited several museums and restaurants to make the experience authentic. We even ate lunch at a dining hall on the campus of Morris Brown College. The trip truly immersed us in southern hospitality and Atlanta's thriving culture.

As we drove around the city, Basheer and Dr. Corttrell Kinney, who was also a chaperone and Morehouse Man, talked about their time in Atlanta as students and all of the fun the city had to offer. Just from riding around the city, I was sold. The skyline was beautiful, the highway was full of traffic, and even on a hot workday, the city buzzed with energy. For many, Atlanta was a place where a black person could be whatever they wanted to be. In Atlanta, opportunity was everywhere.

Many of the natives we spoke to took pride in their city and knew its history very well. Many spoke of the former Mayor Maynard Jackson as one of the primary reasons for Atlanta's success and thriving black community. It also was an opportunity for me to be in the same city many of my favorite rappers were from and talked about in their music so often. At the time, so many popular artists came out of Atlanta that it became an epicenter for black art, talent, and wealth.

Being in Atlanta was the first time I saw black wealth on a large scale. Many bragged about the wealth accumulation in Atlanta and the black people who played a part in it.

During my short visit, I met a black pilot, black professors, black business owners, black CEOs of major companies, several black doctors, and a few black celebrities. These black professionals were everywhere! This was a totally different experience than what I had growing up in Cleveland. Not to say I did not see blacks doing well in Cleveland, but it was nothing like this.

Back home in Cleveland, I only knew a few black people I would have considered successful. These individuals were professionals, had careers, and did not work the blue-collar entry-level jobs no one else wanted due to a lack of education or work experience. The black people who were introduced to us on this trip were different. They were confident and business savvy. They had great ideas and were putting together the pieces of their lives to make their dreams a reality. The professionals in Atlanta had a different type of hustle. They talked positively about gaining a quality education and spoke boldly about black economics. Although I did not understand everything they spoke about, I knew it was different from what I heard every day at home. No one discussed generational wealth at home. Even though people told us we could become doctors or lawyers, we never saw anyone who looked like us or came from similar circumstances as we did achieve this level of success. There was a lack of representation. But, after this trip, none of us could ever make that excuse again.

The conversations that continued at Morehouse were no different. From the moment we stepped off the bus in front of the Walter E. Massey Leadership Center, I felt like I was in a Different World. The campus was not as jam-packed as I thought it would be. Most students who were not participating in commencement ceremonies had already gone home for the summer. For the most part, only the graduating seniors remained. In hindsight, that meant we were blessed with the opportunity to see some of the best Morehouse College had to offer. Everyone moved swiftly as they sauntered around the campus. In their three-piece suits and Stacy Adam's hard bottoms, they crossed the campus back and forth, ensuring all was squared away in preparation for their big day. These brothers were tailored to the tee. They were fly, and you could tell this high-class sense of fashion was the standard on the campus.

As we maneuvered through our campus tour, we were consistently greeted by the college students and faculty. They spoke eloquently about Morehouse and their experiences there. Each person was knowledgeable of the campus and its history. They could tell you when the building was built, who it was named after, and their contributions to the campus. Each monument and gravesite resting upon the campus held significant meaning. There was a statue of Dr. King cemented firmly on campus, but in the eyes of many, it paled in comparison to the entombed monument honoring the 6th President of Morehouse College, Dr. Benjamin Elijah Mays. During my trip and my studies at Morehouse College, I have heard many say that Dr. Mayes is the single most important person in the college's history. He served as a mentor to Dr. King and many other students at Morehouse. During his 27th year tenure as president, he made Morehouse financially secure, academically competitive, and quadrupled enrollment, turning Morehouse into the institution it is known to be today. The young men from Morehouse provided so much wisdom. When speaking with them, they all introduced themselves the same way as if it were rehearsed. They had different names, were from different places, and did different things, but the introduction was always crisp, precise, and uniform. The soon to be college graduates spoke of academics but gave advice more pertinent to success in the real world. One young man, in particular, spoke to us about the importance of friendships and relationship building. He told us our futures would be determined by our five best friends and the books we read. After all those years, the old saying, "Birds of a feather flock together," made sense. He messaged to us that to be successful, we must surround ourselves with successful people. Another gentleman spoke about the importance of being rich. Not rich in terms of capital gain, but rich in terms of spirit, morale, and belief. From our conversation, I learned that being poor was a state of mind. Those that were truly P.O.O.R are those who pass over opportunities repeatedly.

I had never met a group of men, black men, who were not so much older than myself, so focused and prepared for their futures. I never saw guys my age back home wearing suits or starting businesses. It was the same thing every day in the hood: fast money, drugs, and death. I knew then that I wanted something different for my life. Being on Morehouse's Campus solidified it. Like nothing else before, these Morehouse Men intrigued me. I looked forward to returning to the campus each day to meet someone new, shake a new hand, or witness another ceremony the soon-to-be graduates had to participate in. I could not believe all of the knowledge I was gaining and how reinvigorated I was to receive it. I took everything said on the trip literally. I spoke to my roommates at night about the changes we would make in our lives going forward. I felt I learned more in a week than I learned my entire school career. I was definitely drinking the Kool-Aid, and when I made it to campus the next day, I planned to ask someone what made Morehouse College so unique.

Mr. Roberts required us to keep a journal and take copious notes of the things we saw and the information we received. At the end of each night, we were required to write a journal entry about the day's experience and what would change about our life going forward. My journal entries would be 3 to 4 pages long. I had a lot to write and talk about. I would even write poems in my journal to express the way I felt about the trip.

Past, Present, Future

As I open my eyes
I see no future
Just more crooked cops and prosecutors
More junkies and fathers being losers
More like fathers not being fathers
And mothers abandoning daughters
Well, more like mothers not being mothers
And brothers are still killing brothers
More criticizing the situation of others
It seems that the 21st century doesn't breed many lovers
It seems we've been cursed since the landing of Jamestown
But I can remember the teachings of James Brown

Just to see him get down
See, I remember the time like Michael side
By Any Means Necessary like Malcolm did
So back then, it was never about how hard you could shake your dreads
Or how quick we can make the bread
It was about the next generation of kids
But see, now we've lost sight
Because we've lost our fight
We used to march for our rights
But now we just catch the first flight
But remember
There are always snakes on the plane
You would only get on if insane
But, you can only play chess if you understand the game
You cannot cherish life if you do not understand its gains
And you cannot appreciate death if you do not understand the pain
Living out the dream of Dr. Mays, you see
My vision is for healing my communities
So your lack of foresight is not phasing me
But if I do not succeed
Then they're praising me
But I strive in controversy because of the village that is raising me
Nope, I'm not hardly done
Because I will not dry out like a Raisin in the Sun
Because I do it for the lady who is raising the son
And I do it for the one who gave His only begotten son
I do it for the sake of my conscience
Malcolm spoke the truth so, X out the nonsense
No time to be passive, I have to save my community

And never let anyone call you impoverished

Because you're only P.O.O.R. if you pass over opportunities repeatedly

Yes, the flow is cold like Ice Cubes

But it was never All About the Benjamins

The world is calling for our help

Are you listening

We used to be hung like strange fruit

The white pointed hoods were a detriment to our kind

But now it seems to me that we are color blind

Actual and verbal missiles from mouths and pistols

Are taking the place of the segregated system

So it's symbolic that I shoot bullets of knowledge

We started chasing that cash money and ended up on the plantation

13% percent of America but over 70% of the prison population

The game wasn't designed for us to win

And it's blatant

Mr. Roberts coordinated the trip beautifully, yet some things that transpired were merely by the grace of the creator. We were definitely in the right place at the right time. As the week drew to a close, the campus became lively as the Baccalaureate and Commencement Ceremonies were held on Saturday and Sunday, respectively. The Friday before the commencement, we toured the campus with one of the college's instructional deans. Since the trip started, Mr. Roberts would have all the students and chaperones wear the same outfit. On this particular day, we were required to wear khaki pants and a Maroon shirt that read, "From Cleveland to the Morehouse College Commencement Ceremony

2008." On the back, it read, "To Be Continued." If Mr. Roberts could have had it his way, he would have made us all coordinate and wear the same shoes, too. He wanted to make sure we looked as uniformed as possible. Although the trip was about the young men graduating from Morehouse, it was also an opportunity for us to gain positive exposure. I did not truly understand the impact of being dressed alike. On the trip, Mr. Roberts would always emphasize we were one team, and we had one sound. He would say to us, "If one of us looks bad, then we all look bad," and no one was going to "look bad" under his supervision.

As the tour came to a close, we took pictures and recorded videos in front of one of the dormitories. This was our routine at every stop. In the videos, we would thank the people who made the trip possible. We thanked Ohio Governor Ted Strictland, state Senator C.J. Prentiss, CEO of Cleveland Metropolitan schools, Dr. Eugene Sanders, and a host of others. I think Mr. Roberts threw in some names along the way for extra recognition. After a while, all of us hated making these video recordings. Trying to coordinate a photo and synchronized video with all of us on the same page was extremely daunting in the 96 degrees Georgia summer heat. Nevertheless, we would stand there until we got it right. Mr. Roberts made sure of it.

Although many of the dormitories on campus held legacy to their name, the last dorm we took a picture in front of was significant. It was the first building on the campus of Morehouse College, and was said to be the residence hall of the Rev. Dr. Martin Luther King, Jr. We lined up on the steps in rows, shortest to tallest, left to right, each taking the next available step with Mr. Roberts and our cameraman coordinating the photo. These pictures would be used as documentation of our legendary trip to Atlanta and all we experienced there. As we finished our recordings, we said our goodbyes to the Dean, who had so graciously taken his time to impart wisdom to us during our visit. He thanked us all for visiting the institution and, as a proud Morehouse alum himself, recommended we all consider Morehouse a top option for our collegiate studies. He shook our hands and asked if we had any final questions. I knew this was the opportunity I had been waiting for, and I would not waste it. My hand instantly shot into the air, eager to ask the question that had been running through my mind for days. "What makes Morehouse College so unique?" I asked.

He looked at me puzzled, and, in the most uncanny way a Morehouse Man could, the Dean responded, "It's the Morehouse Mystique, son. No one truly knows what it is. But it is forever present, and it lives." He shook a few more hands and then departed. It seemed as if he disappeared into the sunset.

The Baccalaureate Ceremony was long and by far the least exciting moment of the trip. Although filled with people, the campus was quiet, waiting to be awakened from its slumber on the big day. Mr. Roberts once again had us in uniform. At the ceremony, we wore Khaki pants, a collared long sleeve dress shirt, and a black vest that had B.R.I.C.K. arched over a man wearing a cap and gown. B.R.I.C.K. stood for Brotherhood, Respect, Intelligence, Conduct, and Knowledge. It was a mentoring program started in 1996 by Mr. Roberts for young men in Cleveland. The program had many successes. Basheer was one of the program's notable alumni, along with a host of others. Later on, I also became a formal member of the B.R.I.C.K. Program and used its five principles to elevate my life.

We spent the majority of our Saturday on the campus, watching the seniors rehearse for the ceremony. We took some photos of the graduates who we had the pleasure of meeting during our trip. I still have many of those pictures, and I often go back to look at them. They remind me of my transition from being a wannabe to a Man of Morehouse to ultimately graduating and becoming a Morehouse Man. Dressed in our sweaters and neck-ties, many of the students focused their attention on us, letting us know if this (the graduation) was something we wanted to experience, we would have to work hard over the next eight years to see it happen. That night when we left the campus, I was exhausted. I felt as if I had been practicing for my graduation. The next day would be the Commencement, the finale we had all been waiting for. Mr. Roberts was so enthusiastic. He paced back and forth, walked in circles, and continuously kept saying small mantras to himself. He did not speak loud enough for anyone to hear him, but whatever he was saying to himself held importance. Occasionally, he would say aloud, "It's showtime, gentleman."

The day of the graduation was intense. Mr. Roberts woke everyone up at 5 AM to ensure we were on time and fine for the Commencement. The pristine suits were wonderfully tailored to fit our silhouettes, and we could not wait for everyone to see us looking dapper. Mr. Roberts went around to each of our hotel rooms to ensure our clothes were ironed, pressed, and clean. Luckily for me, I brought an extra white collared shirt because the other had developed a dirt ring around the neck from all of my moving and sweating. For those who did not have extra shirts, Mr. Roberts gave them a loaner. He was always overly prepared. Our suits were clean, and our pants were creased so hard, we could barely bend at the knee. Mr. Roberts required everyone to meet him outside in the parking lot at 6:15 AM sharp. When we all arrived, he had us stand in a single file line as he examined our uniforms before we boarded the bus. In my humble opinion, we outdressed some of the Morehouse Men that day.

On the bus ride to Morehouse, Mr. Roberts and Basheer gave us motivational talks and reminded us that all eyes would be on us; it was our time to shine.

We arrived at the campus the same way we had done before, offboarding the charter bus in front of the Walter E. Massey Leadership Building. This time, the campus was full of people. Crowds of people filled the streets, and we grasped their attention as we got off the bus. Mr. Roberts instructed us to line up on the left side of the street, and we would walk in unison to the legendary Brown Street that splits Morehouse's campus in two. Brown Street led to Century Campus, where Dr. Mays stood to watch the graduates cement themselves in the history books of great Morehouse Men. The thought sent chills down my spine.

As we walked inside the gates of Morehouse College, the graduates' families and friends began to walk over to us. They inquired about who we were, what we were doing, and where we were headed. We proudly told them we were from Cleveland, OH, and we were there to experience the graduation of young black men who looked like us. They applauded us, hugged us, shook our hands, and took our photos. They even went as far as to ask for some of our autographs. They did not know us at all but demanded us not to give up and to stay on the path of excellence.

Immediately, I began to feel conflicted. As I stood there accepting recognition for embodying black excellence, I did not feel I had done anything to receive praise. I wanted to tell them that I was not deserving of their kind words, thoughtful gestures, worship, and embrace. I wanted to tell them that the suit and tie were all a facade. They needed to know I wasn't the person they thought I was. I wanted to inform them that I was a fake. Deep down inside, I knew I wasn't working my hardest in school. I knew my grades were far below average, and I still had not made a genuine commitment to my future success. However, I remained silent, smiled, and politely thanked our admirers. While I was drinking the Kool-aid, I wasn't performing to the standard of a future Morehouse Man, and those thoughts would haunt me for many years to come.

As we lined up on the sidewalk behind the gates protecting Brown Street, we all waited in anticipation for the ceremonies to begin. A loud bell resounded in the air, then the playing of African drums and the festivities were underway. When the drummers turned off of Westview Drive onto Brown Street, everyone began to clap and cheer. There were roars of excitement from families and friends who had come to see the hard work of their young men. Following the procession were a group of gentlemen dressed in fine suits. They were all wearing white straw top hats that bore a maroon band with the words, Morehouse Alumnus. Each group of men walked behind a banner representing their respective graduating class. There were several gentlemen there celebrating their 65th and 70th-year anniversaries. I even witnessed two men being pushed in wheelchairs up Brown Street by two other Morehouse Men. Such brotherhood and deference. It was a beautiful sight to see.

As they passed, we applauded them, and after examining our debonair attire, they did the same in return. I thought it was very classy of those accomplished men to take a moment during their time to acknowledge us. They shook our hands and let us know all of this could be ours if we so chose. My feelings of guilt and shame set in again. I hated the affection they gave me, and I did not know if they would truly accept me for who I was — a pretender. I immediately wanted to change who I was. I did not want to be another person; I just wanted to be a better version of myself. I wanted to be worthy of all of the admiration.

Another roar came from the crowd. The graduates had finally made it to the gates and were taking their legendary walk from Brown Street to Century Campus. The crowd who awaited them was losing it, ourselves included. Laughs, tears of joy, and pain all began to fall from the graduates and families as they made their way up the hill. Seeing waves of black men dressed in caps, gowns, and regalia, marching to the sounds of the drums impacted me deeply. They smiled and waved at their families, many with tears in their eyes, as they knew they had accomplished something great. It was the most extraordinary thing I had seen in all of my years.

The graduates were different shades of black and

brown, from different walks of life, but they were all bound by their commitment to black excellence. This is what made Morehouse so special. Nowhere else in the world could you witness 500 African American men graduate from college and witness them make the transition into the rest of their lives. As the graduates passed, everyone gathered behind them to make their way to campus to finish the rest of the ceremony and witness the awarding of degrees. As each name was called, I began to envision myself being one of the Morehouse graduates, walking across the stage as people cheered me on. The smiles of accomplishment pressed upon their faces will never leave me. It seemed to be the most glorious day of their lives. Many of them grew into men during their time at Morehouse. The trials, tribulations, lessons learned, and friendships built would grant them a lifetime of memories. For those who allowed Mother Morehouse to pass through them, this day embodied the matriculation and progression to true manhood.

The campus, so soft and quiet the day before, was now filled with energy and enthusiasm. The students walked across the stage and graduated, some with honors. As some names were announced, the Master of Ceremonies would say, Summa Cum Laude, Magna Cum Laude, or Cum Laude. Later, some graduates who were not designated by the college as honors students said they graduated "thank-you Laude," praising the creator for helping them along their academic journey. Regardless of the journey each young man had to take to achieve this goal, on this day, they all sat as brothers and recognized each other as the esteemed Morehouse College Graduating Class of 2008. After the ceremony, the newly minted Morehouse Men greeted their families and friends and made plans to celebrate their accomplishments that evening. On the other hand, we headed to dinner, then back to the hotel to prepare for our departure to Cleveland.

Our final night at the hotel was an emotional one. In our group session, many of us cried about the impact the day had on us and what it meant for our futures. Mr. Roberts spoke passionately about his intention for the trip that evening. Coming from the communities we come from, he understood the impact that a lack of role models and positive reinforcement could have on young men. Mr. Roberts wanted to make sure that after this trip, without a doubt, we could all say we knew there was a better life out there for us. He wanted us to know that education was the absolute and only way to achieve legitimate freedom. Frankly speaking, one trip changed everything about the way I viewed my life. Everything I thought I ever desired suddenly changed. After that week in Atlanta, I wanted to be a Morehouse Man, and I was willing to do anything to see it happen.

The next morning, we headed to the airport extremely exhausted but fulfilled. The same obstacles facing us before at the airport were no longer apparent. There was no fear in our eyes, only determination, and purpose. We were eager to get home to display all we had learned, and little did we know, the whole city awaited our return to hear of the experience. When we returned home, our families picked us up from Martin Luther King Jr. High School. Our parents who missed us desperately rushed to the bus to hug the boys they had sent on a trip to Atlanta a week before. However, those boys were gone forever; the trip to Atlanta had transformed us into young men. Over the next several weeks, I had the opportunity to talk to several newspapers and participate in countless interviews about my experience on the trip. Mr. Roberts and the other chaperones had identified me as one of the student leaders on the trip, so a lot of attention and recognition came my way.

When I returned to school, I was a new person. I changed everything about my style. I no longer wanted to follow the traditional school uniform. I began to wear suits and ties to school every day. Since I only owned one suit, I began to raid my grandfather's closet for any old dress clothes and other items he owned. Going through the closets in my grandparents' attic, I found enough clothing to last me until I could begin to draft a more professional wardrobe. In the process of clothes hunting, I noticed my grandfather was a pretty dapper guy. He owned many classic suits that added character to my attire. Instead of my typical urban attire, I dressed business casual for the remainder of my high school career. I did my best to emulate what I saw in the Morehouse Men in Atlanta. I even began to coin myself a Morehouse Man and told everyone that I would attend Morehouse College in Atlanta.

PART SIX

OLD HABITS DIE HARD

W hen we returned from Atlanta, there were only three weeks left in the school year. Though I was committed to doing better, I did not have enough time to significantly raise my grades. Nevertheless, freshman year ended on a higher note academically, but nothing like what would be expected to become a Morehouse Man. My fourth quarter grade point average was 2.7, the highest I had earned in years. I did not lack the intelligence to perform well in school; I was just lazy and undetermined. Until I attended the trip to Morehouse College, I had no reason to take school seriously. I had never envisioned myself going to college or having a legitimate career. I planned to graduate from high school and get a job. That would be the thick of it.

I felt really good about earning a 2.7 GPA for the last semester. For the amount of work I completed in a short amount of time, I felt accomplished. I would brag to my friends about how easy the work was and how it took me no time to bring my grades to just above average. None of them had better grades than I did, so I stood as the intelligent one with no one willing to challenge my boasting. In ignorance,

I thought I would start my sophomore year with a 2.7. I did not factor in my lackadaisical performance at the beginning of the year, so my cumulative grade point average was 2.3. I had no concept of a cumulative GPA. In middle school, our GPA wasn't cumulative, and it reset every quarter. Dr. Corttrell Kinney, who would begin to mentor me daily, made me aware of the importance of my cumulative GPA. Dr. Kinney consistently challenged me to raise my grades and work hard all of the time, not just some of the time. He rained on my parade anytime he felt I was getting a little too egotistical. There were many times during my high school career where Dr. Kinney would say I was "feeling myself too much," having accomplished so little.

Even at my most stubborn times, Dr. Kinney never gave up on me. One night, an argument with Dr. Kinney about my grades made me so angry that I challenged him to a fistfight right in my driveway. He always knew what buttons to push to get me going. The conviction I felt also played a part in my frustration; I knew what he was saying was right. I had not yet accomplished anything, and at the rate I was working, I would not. Even after the extreme lack of respect I showed him, Dr. Kinney stood by my side. He made sure I held to the promise I had made myself and so many others.

During my sophomore year of high school, I was blessed to accumulate many mentors. After the trip to Atlanta, I was identified as a student with a bright future, and my mentors began to pour into me regularly. They all provided me with the different skills I would need to be successful in life. My sister taught me the importance of creativity. My mother taught me the importance of having self-respect. Mr. Golden taught me how to set goals and manage my time. Basheer taught me the importance of self-worth, self-identification, and effective communication. Mr. Roberts encouraged me to have a vision for my life, be open-minded, and be willing to learn.

Along with all of those things, Dr. Corttrell Kinney ensured I understood the importance of self-promotion, discipline, and consistency. He also taught me the imperativeness of having an unrelenting work ethic. Most importantly, Dr. Kinney showed me how to make money. He would drill into my brain, day in and day out, the concept of these skills and the importance of doing excellent work.

From 10th grade until the day I graduated, I was with Dr. Kinney in some way. He served as my tutor and helped me get on the correct academic path. As I worked with Dr. Kinney, he began to identify what he would call 'gaps in my package.' I had poor study habits, and I wasn't willing to go the extra mile when it came to my work. I would always do the bare minimum, never pushing myself to go beyond what was asked. He found me to be inconsistent, only willing to work hard when I felt like it — not when it was required. He discovered that although I was very motivated, I lacked discipline. My lack of discipline caused me to miss deadlines or not complete tasks. No matter how much I said I would be a Morehouse Man, my current commitment level would not get me there.

For me, Dr. Kinney was a "Debbie Downer," as nothing I ever did would impress him. Anytime I told him something I did, he replied, "Okay. And? That's what you're supposed to do." Dr. Kinney was a man of high expectations and a very talented academic himself. He graduated top of his class from John Hay High School in Cleveland, OH. He graduated with high honors from Morehouse College with a bachelor's degree in biology. He served as a research scientist for one of the major hospitals in the country's northeast region. To top it all off, he received his Ph.D. in Physiology and Biophysics from Case Western Reserve University by 28. He was a true genius — the real deal.

I was most impressed with his work capacity. Dr. Kinney was the first person I knew to openly have several different streams of income. He owned real estate, a company, and had fruitful investments. He was also a scientist, held several board of directors positions with various organizations, and mentored and tutored students. He was extremely passionate about all of his endeavors and relentless when it came to completing a task. He would slave over an assignment for hours at a time until it was complete. If there was information he needed to know, he would beat it into his brain, constantly revisiting the information as if it would run away from him if he did not continuously check for it. He would often work into the wee hours of the morning, and only the illumination of his laptop screen brought light to the room.

My mother, who was skeptical of just about everything initially, did not approve of my growing relationship with Dr. Kinney. She was not fond of me spending most of my time after school with him and attending late-night events with him. During my sophomore year, I also decided to join the Glenville High School Wrestling and Golf Teams, headed by coach Gregory Dodson and Coach Allan Cabiness, respectively. With all of these new activities going on, I spent very little time at home. My mother's house became a place where I only rested my head and prepare for the next day. My mother began to scorn me for being away from home so much. She felt I was slacking on my home responsibilities, so she overloaded me with chores. There were times when she prevented me from going to events because she did not "feel comfortable" with me spending so much time with Dr. Kinney and my other mentors. At times, we would argue and fight about her discomfort, sometimes, right in front of my mentors. It was embarrassing trying to convince my mother that my mentors meant well by me. By the middle of my junior year, my mother began to realize the serious young man I was becoming. After seeing the impact my mentors had on my life, she understood that in addition to her hard work, I needed positive male influence.

Mr. Golden and Mr. Roberts gave me access to things happening around the school district. Dr. Kinney was my introduction to many of the resources and opportunities greater Cleveland had to offer. Over several years, Dr. Kinney taught me the art of networking by dragging me to what felt like every professional event in Cleveland. Thanks to Dr. Kinney, as a high school student, I attended some of the most elegant banquets and symposiums with top movers and shakers from around the city. Most of the time, we would not even have tickets for the event. Dr. Kinney would call me hours before an event and tell me to get dressed because he was on his way. Someway, somehow, Dr. Kinney would get us access to the event, secure a table, and maneuver an opportunity to speak. He would often bring several other mentees along for the trip. I was always concerned with how he navigated his way into events, as I considered it freeloading. I worried about being denied access and facing the embarrassment of being turned away. Dr. Kinney did not care about any of that. He would often say, "Come on now. Think about it. Do you think they are going to turn away four young black men in suits? That would be insane. Could you imagine how that would look?" Although I did not always agree with Dr. Kinney's antics, he was right. Thankfully, people felt the same way he did, and we were never denied entry or a seat at the table. The event organizers were always impressed by a group of young men invested in their futures.

Being at these events, I began to identify organizations and people who were of the caliber of those I met while in Atlanta. There were many names and faces, but this conglomerate of black people was small as I saw the same people at different events around the city. Each event would highlight a new face, a new name, and a new organization. After attending the first few events, the excitement of going left me, and I would put up a fight anytime it was time for us to attend. I would only want to attend the events I wanted to attend and would only be open to meeting new people if I felt like it. Dr. Kinney would argue me into submission and demanded me to make new contacts while at events. I do not know why I was so stubborn or what made me so annoyed. He would always say, "One day, you may need some of these people," and he turned out to be right. All of the relationships I built would eventually help to propel me to Morehouse College. I did not know it at the time, but Dr. Kinney set me up to win in the long run.

One particular morning after participating in a youth

symposium Basheer hosted, he invited me to be on his radio show. This would be my first time being live on the air, and I wanted to make sure I sounded as intelligent as possible. This was a big deal for me as I loved being on the microphone and in the spotlight. I got an excuse from school that morning to miss half the day. Dr. Kinney gave me a ride to the radio station, and when I got there, I was greeted by the radio staff. Being welcomed so warmly by their team made me feel like a big deal. They led me into the waiting room, offered me snacks and beverages, and told me Basheer would be with me in a moment. Dr. Kinney and I sat in the waiting room silently. I was extremely nervous and could not formulate many words. Dr. Kinney broke the silence, "You ready?" I shook my head yes, as I grew accustomed to saying I was okay when I actually wasn't. Dr. Kinney then followed up with another question. "Do you know what you are going to say?" I shook my head no, but did not utter a word. "I hope you have more than that to say when you get on the air," he replied. He and I expressed the same sentiments as I awaited Basheer to enter the room. The longer I waited, the more my anxiety grew.

After another five or so minutes, Basheer's radio manager walked in and introduced herself. "You must be Cedric?" she said as she moved in to embrace me. Her comforting hug seemed to melt all my fears away. She gestured for me to follow her and led me out of the cold waiting area into a room across the hall. There was a window where I could see Basheer on air through the glass and hear what he was saying on a separate headset. She began to prep me on what to do once I was on the air. She informed me that Basheer would ask me a series of questions and that I should answer them as honestly as possible. His manager told me to treat the interaction like a dialogue. She also let me know there would be thousands of people listening to what I said, and if I got stuck, Basheer would be there to assist me. She assured me there would be nothing to worry about. This subsided my anxiety slightly, but it would not hold for long.

During a lengthy commercial break, Basheer got up from his studio chair and grabbed me from the other room. He seemed so excited to see me and was even more eager to get me on the show. "Little Bro! What's going on?" he said. "Are you ready for the show? You're going to do great."

"Yeah, I'm ready. Let's do it," I responded. He shook my hand, and we headed into another room. Though it only took us five seconds to walk from one room to the next, it felt like an eternity. I felt like everything was moving in slow motion. My breathing grew heavy, my palms turned sweaty, my knees buckled, and my legs started to feel like spaghetti noodles. I was shaken, but I could not let Basheer know it.

A large glass window allowed you to see inside the studio. There were several chairs and a large table covered in newspapers Basheer had been flipping through that morning. The walls were padded for soundproofing, and there were professional microphones attached to stands that came out of the tables. For the first time in my life, I was in a professional studio. I gathered myself and gave myself a personal pep talk as I did not want to ruin my moment due to fear.

Basheer waited for another commercial break before introducing me on the air. In the meantime, he got me set up with a headset and ensured my microphone was working properly. When the commercial break was near the end, Basheer took his seat, placed his headset over his crown, and gave me a slight smile and head nod. I knew we were about to begin. The commercial ended, and Basheer jumped into radio mode:

BASHEER: "What's going on, family. It's your brother, Basheer Jones. I hope all is well and welcome back to the Basheer Jones and Company Morning Show. This morning, I am very excited to have a special guest on the air with us today. Today, I have with us a young brother by the name of Cedric Thorbes, who is a sophomore at Glenville High School. Cedric, how are you doing this morning?"

ME: "I'm doing well. Thank you."

BASHEER: "I met this young brother several months ago and had the opportunity to take Cedric and a group of young men on a tour of Morehouse College for their commencement ceremony. It was a great trip, and I feel like it truly impacted the lives of the young men who went. Cedric, it's good to see you again, and welcome to the show."

ME: "Thank you so much for having me."

Basheer began to ask me a series of questions just as the woman from the other room told me he would. He asked about the trip, its impact, and where I saw myself in the next ten years, given all the opportunities I had received. I spoke boldly about my aspirations and my goals in life. That morning on Basheer's talk show, I told over one hundred thousand people I had dreams of attending Morehouse College and that I would one day be a Morehouse Man. Listeners called the show to ask me a few questions as well. Others called to congratulate me on a job well done and encouraged my path to success. After about a 30-minute interview, Basheer thanked me for joining his show and proudly told everyone I had to leave to return to school for my academics. Before I was dismissed, Basheer asked me for one more thing.

> **BASHEER:** Before we let this young brother leave, I'm going to ask him to provide us with a little gift. This young brother has the gift of the spoken word, and I'm going to ask him to share some of his powerful words with us. Let's go, Cedric. Give us what you got.

I was stunned, caught off guard, and baffled. They never mentioned anything about reciting a poem. I felt like I had been set up, and Basheer was trying to put pressure on me. I was unprepared and did not know what to recite on the show. I started to recite the only poem I had converted to memory. It was a poem I had written several months prior.

My Society

I was characterized by my skin color
And put against people with different exchanges
To them, the average black man is brainless
Nameless with no identity
They built the jail to get rid of me
No sensitivity I was criticized by the public

Hatred from the attic to basement
But I must face it
My race I will never disgrace it
God sent me to give this world a facelift
Something like me with this much prestige is hard to come by
But when they see me and my clan of young black men
It's always, not to be mean but do not you guys play for a basketball team
But since my level of thinking is higher, I keep moving
But if I told the world I was inspired to be a writer
They would call me a liar
All eyes on me as I walk away as if I set the world on fire
Because I initiated the flame when I opened my eyes up
Like the Cavaliers say, "Man, we all must rise up!"
Whether it's death or prison
They're trying to divide us
They would never picture me to be a significant part of history
Because I was just another statistic
That was taken over by the government
Do not really care about the Democrats or the Republicans
I'm not a politician
I just wish every time I turn on the news
I do not have to hear about another one of my black brothers missing
Or how your boy's in jail and how much you miss him
You see, I'm not a saint, but we're all doing too much sinning
You see, no, I'm no Baptist
But where was the backup
When they sentenced me to prison
Where was the backup when I needed a place to be living
You see, the streets are doing the crimes

But, the government's doing the killing
Because they're making a killing off the boys in the penitentiary
It's so major they have them working hard labor like this was slavery
This is the 2008 version of slavery
It's so easy to go to jail and have your life to be ruined
As a matter of fact, it's so easy that a caveman can do it
So go ahead
Take your life and use it and abuse it and you'll lose it
Because there was no sensitivity
When they built the jail to get rid of me.

When I finished, everyone in earshot of the poem was in awe. Listeners called the station, applauding what I had done and saying how we needed more positive young black men in our communities. I felt so powerful at that moment. So many people were influenced by my words and the sound of my voice. Even though it was not in person, it was the first time I had performed in front of a large audience. I did well, but I hated performing my poetry in public. For me, poetry was still very different from rap. I appreciated the art form. I respected those who took the time to develop and cultivate the craft. But performing poetry in public just wasn't my thing. Most people still did not know I did spoken word; I tried my best to keep it under wraps. Yet, on that day, with thousands of people listening, the secret was out: I could spit poetry.

Dr. Kinney stood in the doorway, astonished at what he had witnessed. Eyes big and mouth open, I could tell I intrigued him on a different level. For the longest time, he had no clue I wrote poetry. He had never asked about it, and

I never mentioned it. He knew I rapped, but poetry seemed to be held in higher regard for him — and everyone else, quite frankly. There was something about spoken word that garnered people's attention. Exiting the studio, I was given handshakes and fist bumps. Dr. Kinney was the only person who did not embrace me upon my departure. He remained in silence the entire way to the car.

Once we got in the car, Dr. Kinney did not start the car immediately. He sat in deep thought and stared at me for a moment. "You do poetry?" he inquired. "Why did not you tell me you did poetry? I cannot believe you. You did not say anything, and you're actually pretty good. You just were not going to say anything about it?"

"It's not that big of a deal. I do not like doing poetry anyway. I just did it because I got put on blast." I replied.

"But you're really good. Do you know how much money you could be making from doing spoken word? I wish I were gifted like that. I would perform poetry everywhere I went." Dr. Kinney said. I did not respond. I did not want to talk about it, but that did not prevent him from talking about it the whole ride back to school.

When I returned to campus, several of the staff members had heard me on air. They expressed how impressed they were with how I conducted myself in the interview and told me I did extremely well on the poem. It was like they saw me in a new light — as if they noticed me for the first time. I embraced this newfound popularity. I was ecstatic at all of the attention I was receiving. More importantly, I was receiving attention for being a positive student. From that day forward, school became a vibrant place where I felt loved, welcomed, and respected. I began to love spending time in school and with my teachers. I began to take my course work seriously, and Dr. Kinney was there every step of the way to ensure my grades did not slip. As a part of the golf and wrestling teams, I gained new friends who were also dedicated to their studies.

Thanks to the CTAG program, I met many of my closest friends from around the school district and Co-Captain of the golf team, Perry Wyatt. In my new group of friends, I was no longer the smartest student. My 2.3 grade point average fell short in comparison to Perry's whopping 4.0. Perry would become a close friend in high school by being my biggest competition on the golf course and in the classroom. I knew I would never be able to catch up to Perry in terms of cumulative grade point average, so I made sure I battled him relentlessly each quarter.

Each quarter, I would lose as Perry would continue to maintain his perfect grade point average. Although I would not achieve a higher GPA than Perry until the final quarter of our senior year, he consistently challenged me to raise my efforts in class. Work concepts seemed to come easy to Perry. He was a genius in math and an overachiever in every other subject. For me, it was a little different. I struggled with math, and I hated science. I was always very intrigued by history and excelled in it. I loved to read and write due to my excessive rap habit, so English class was a strong suit for me. To get a good grade in math, I had to work hard. This is why I always felt personally attacked when Dr. Kinney would scorn me for not having higher grades. As I strived to excel academically, I became more consistent with my poetry writing, and over the years, I got better.

Why We Cannot Wait

A man who was murdered on the balcony
For speaking words of equality
Is now our mogul for peace and serenity
Who gave hope to the impoverished
And for those who are nothing to become accomplishments
A state of mind not to be violent
Even against discrimination
Even against segregation
We knew change would not happen overnight
So we had to be patient
Not being physical but using his brain made him one of the most
dangerous men in the nation
But to serve his people was Dr. King's obligation
But now we are facing a new time with different issues
So we need a new leader to guide us through
Through all the pain, the wars, and the drama
A change can come with President Obama
To lead us in a positive direction
We all made a change with the presidential election
We need change, no substitutions
We've suffered through eight years of problems
Let's start making some solutions.
But Why We Cannot Wait?
Because we're tired of seeing the same face
We need to make a difference before it's too late
Time to make a change because we know our own fate
Because America, now, is a disgrace
How would they rather send us to jail than to give us knowledge
Build multi-million dollar prisons but will not send us to college

Foreclosure on homes
Just another neighborhood to be impoverished
I do not think this was the dream of the gentleman from Morehouse
College
We the people of the United States, in order to form a more perfect
union
Must come together to figure out which battles we are losing
Is it the one overseas?
Or is it the one at home with our school system, economic system,
poverty, and disease
We heard the speech I Have a Dream from Dr. King
Which made us all patient
Now we hear President Obama's speech of Inauguration
But why we cannot wait?
Because we feel hopeless
But we know we are not worthless
Dr. King had a dream
So Obama can have purpose

The ones I liked I would keep, and the others, I would throw in the trash. Dr. Kinney would consistently tell me to keep all my poems, and that one day, my poems may be worth some money. I did not listen. I can say I threw away over 50 poems. I wasn't patient enough to take them through the editing process. Looking back, I definitely let go of some solid material that would still hold precedence today. Yet, I feel what I kept and what I continue to create is a true testament to my dedication to the craft.

After hearing me recite poetry at the radio station, Dr. Kinney always requested me to do spoken word everywhere we went. I would constantly refuse. He tried to convince me to perform at large events, small family gatherings, church events, any place my voice could be heard. I would consistently turn him down. I have argued with Dr. Kinney in front of many people on several occasions about performing. He began to attribute my stubbornness to the artist in me and said that most artists he knew were always very particular and wanted to do things their way. Deep down, I knew the real reason why I did not want to perform. I was afraid of being ridiculed, talked about, or criticized. I was also afraid of someone agreeing with my work and holding me accountable for all of the black excellence rhetoric I spoke.

Dr. Kinney would always tell me that in order to be a successful black man, I had to be the total package. With so many strikes against us already, my record had to be squeaky clean across the board. Around this time, Barack Obama was the U.S. President-Elect. He was always the shining example of the total package — a highly educated black man with a beautiful wife and family. There were no scandals tied to President Obama's name, outside children, or true discrepancies about his character. He was extremely handsome and well-spoken. This was the mold Dr. Kinney wanted to shape me after, and he would push this notion every day. He believed success was centered around being a well-rounded person. It wasn't enough for me to speak well or do spoken word. Dr. Kinney wanted me to live out the messages I put in my poetry. He did not want me to suffer from a case of imposter syndrome. "Cedric, the things you say in your poems should be a reflection of your grades and the things you are doing in the community. You cannot be running around here talking about black prosperity and greatness, and you have a 2.5 GPA. It's not going to work. You have to do better," he would say. Over the course of my high school career, I would do better, much better. But during the beginning phase of the transition, as you could imagine, old habits die hard.

One day, Dr. Kinney and I visited a church of one of the pastors he did community work with around the city. Although always present, we were not the most timely bunch. With so much running around the city, we would sometimes overlap our meetings, escaping one in enough time to make it to the other. That day, we left bright and early to ensure we made it to the church on time. Even with all of our preparation, we still arrived at the sanctuary slightly behind schedule, but in just enough time to fill in the pews in the front of the church. The pastor delivered a captivating sermon that stirred the soul of the congregation. They were hooked on every word he said. Every statement was followed by "Yes, Lord!' and "Amen!" The organist and drummer allowed their instruments to sing to the heavens as the pastor shouted on the stage. Every person was filled with the Holy Spirit and jumped, shouted, and clapped in response. After the sermon, the pastor acknowledged several people in the audience, including Dr. Kinney.

He asked Dr. Kinney to greet the church and say a few words about who he was and the work he did in the community. Of course, Dr. Kinney obliged. He stood, adjusted the buttons on his suit jacket, and made his way to the front of the room. An usher rushed over to hand him a microphone. He introduced himself as a Morehouse

Man would and spoke of his academic achievements. People were always astonished when he mentioned his doctorate credentials. Most people could not pronounce it, and he would have to reiterate it multiple times. After briefly introducing himself, he spoke about the students he mentored, myself included. I sat in the audience, embarrassed as everyone in the church looked at me and applauded Dr. Kinney. He went on to share the many accolades of his mentees, past and present. Dr. Kinney had an extensive track record of turning average students into achievers. Then, he turned his attention back on me and my amazing gift of spoken word. He told the congregation about my radio appearance and expressed excitement about the new material I had shared with him in private. Once again, caught off guard, Dr. Kinney invited me to share my poetry with the audience. Everyone cheered, and Dr. Kinney flashed a devilish grin as he knew he had finally won. I was reluctant to stand until the pastor said, "Come on up here, Cedric. Show us what the Lord has blessed you with." I did not want to perform, and Dr. Kinney knew that. But with over 100 people watching, I did not have a choice. I arose from my seat, and the congregation roared again. I walked to the front, aggressively took the microphone from Dr. Kinney, faced the audience, gave them a slight grin, and began to rip off one of my newest pieces of work.

We Are What Hope Looks Like

We represent something different
We represent everything our communities have been missing
So just listen

You see we represent that conscious
That differs from the nonsense
Just to stay positive
Speaking words of wisdom
Just to past the derogative
But you see, we represent our kings
Who walk around in saggy jeans and long hoodies and tees
Just to get the flow of the streets
You see we represent the D-Boy who
Stands and hustles on the corner just to get something to eat
But you see, we have to represent that motherless child
Who has been nothing but let down
So she has no choice but to let down
Her pants just to feel loved
We represent the thug who does nothing but fight and smoke drugs
Just to have his name mentioned on the block
You see we represent the jack boy whose been constantly shot
But we have to represent these young people
Who've been brutally abused by cops
Because we represent a culture that has lost its voltage
Because we've all been tricked
And understand that we've been playing their game for a while
Because they would not give us our 40 acres and a mule
But they gave us a 40 Ounce and a mild
Gave my young ladies babies and gave my young brother 40 cals
Just so they can rob a brother and tell 'em
Get down
Give me everything you got
I want whatever you got in your pockets
And whatever you got in your spot

But then it's time to pay bail
But I wonder how long it will take these egg whites
To connect it back to their yolk
Just to get it through their shells
Now listen
A poetic delinquent's delirium delivers demented demeanors
Drowning, demoralizing, demolishing
Demanding deluded depiction
Deviating detonators not to blow the whole world
Because we represent the struggle
But now it seems our people are out of shape because we let too many squares
In our circles
It's like we are trying to make Stephen's out of Urkel's
And make Laura's out of Myrtle's
But family matters
And we have to recognize that no matter how the window shatters
The glass is always going to point back to you
But it's like we play our game backward
Because we teach our kids that it's cool to be squares like Spongebob
Instead of stars like Patrick
And this poses a problem
Because all we end up doing
Is ending up at Bikini Bottom
Because you see
All the problems happen in the twilight
But we shouldn't have to wait for an eclipse just to get our new moon
My young ladies shouldn't have to be broken down and emotional hurt to go and jump a broom
And young boys shouldn't have to wait till they are being married to

be properly groomed
But it's like we never learned because dad never showed up
And you see, we used to be Rugrats
But now we're all grown up
And that pain of never truly being loved starts to come into place
And that pain is what you see when you look in my face
But even with that pain, I shine so bright
So I can stand here today and say
We are what hope looks like
And we started off as a lump of coal
And they said it would take pressure to mold
Into a diamond
One that is constantly shining
And nothing is ever stopping our glow
Even if Simon said so
And just know
That we'll break through your windows if you will not open the door
But just know we're coming
But you saw us from miles away
Just know that we're coming
Because you see, we represent hope every day
Just know we're coming
Because we do for those who are mentally enslaved
Just know we're coming
Because we do it for the enslaved that are now in graves
Morehouse, we're coming
Because I do it for Benjamin Elijah Mayes
CMSD we're coming
Because through this transformation, it's time for some change

So for all of those who lost a whole lot of hope and a whole lot of faith
Just know we're coming
Because we are what hope looks like

The congregation lost it. People shouted, chanted, and thanked the Lord for my inspirational words and presence. The poem was a hit, but I was so flustered, I just returned to my seat, bowed my head, and barely acknowledged the applause. The reverend walked into the pulpit and said, "Now will not He use you?" To which the crowd responded, "Now yes, He will." I sat and faced front, not turning or making eye contact with anyone but the paster. He spoke to me directly for a moment, then addressed his congregation about the importance of mentorship and bringing someone along with you. He applauded Dr. Kinney for his efforts and took a collection from the church on my behalf. "In the spirit of bringing someone along, we are going to do something from Cedric to keep him going along the path of success. We're going to pass the offering plate around, and you place in it what you feel Cedric deserves for his services." The music played, and the ushers took the collection plate around. As it passed my face, I contributed a dollar because I felt my performance was worth the fee. Shortly after, the service ended, and we followed the pastor to his chambers to count out the money I had earned that morning.

Two-thousand dollars! In less than five minutes of work at the church, I made a little over $2,000. That was the most money I had ever held in my life, and I did not have to steal, rob, kill, or sell drugs for it. It was clean money, and I could not believe how easily I earned it. "I told you, I told you. Did I not tell you? That poetry is a goldmine. People love it," Dr. Kinney said.

I sat in the passenger seat and silently counted the money that had started to burn a hole in my pocket. After that day, I never declined Dr. Kinney's requests for me to perform, and the money and opportunities grew. He helped me set up business cards and a speaker one sheet so that I would look legit when I performed around the city. Dr. Kinney believed in my skills so much that he booked studio time for me to record a poetry CD. Once it was produced, I sold them for $10 at my engagements. I kept quiet about my earnings, but I had more money than the average teenager in my neighborhood. I wasn't financially savvy, so of course, I spent the money on irrelevant things I can not remember. However, the concept of creating products or providing a service to receive compensation was etched in my mind.

PART SEVEN

GETTING IT TOGETHER

Once junior year rolled around, Dr. Kinney and I had a steady daily routine that continued into my senior year. I would attend school in the morning, practice after school, and tackle endeavors with Dr. Kinney in the evening. My body grew accustomed to functioning off a few hours of sleep, but I was always exhausted. Seeing my hard work pay off kept me going. My name began to grow around the city as one of the best poets and one of the school district's top scholars. My accomplishments landed me features in some of the nation's top magazines such as Essence, in addition to local publications around the city. Organizations frequently reached out to Dr. Kinney to book me for speaking engagements. I was on the "banquet campaign" as Coach Dotson called it. At wrestling practice, he would ridicule my weight gain and blame it all on those banquet meals. Nevertheless, Dr. Kinney and I continued to show up at events. Each time, I would show out and continue to make a name for myself. I wasn't paid for every event. Dr. Kinney believed I should do some events for free. He advised that since I was still new on the scene, the exposure and experience I gained would be worth more than the money. He was right. In many ways, Dr. Kinney served as my manager, although he never took any credit or any portions of my earnings.

As I learned how to put myself out there, Dr. Kinney encouraged me to step it up a notch. If I wanted to make a splash and compete with some of the world's most talented students, I would have to be more involved in the community. Many of the organizations I performed for had youth sectors with leadership councils and executive board positions. Dr. Kinney encouraged me to join as many of these organizations as possible and to run for the highest available leadership position. This time around, I did not argue with him. I took his advice, joined various organizations around the city as an interested general member, and caught on to the concepts of the organizations quickly. By senior year, I had become the youth president of several very prominent organizations in Cleveland. I served as president of the Cleveland NAACP Youth Council, Cleveland Youth Chapter President of the Southern Leadership Conference, Youth President of The B.R.I.C.K. Program, and Glenville High School Senior Class President. I also served as a Student Ambassador for the Closing the Achievement Gap Program (CTAG) on the district level. This position allowed me to interact with the school district's executive leadership team. I often went to the school board and had random encounters and lunch dates with the superintendent and deputy chiefs of the district. With all my new resources, I began hosting events in my school and around the city. I hosted poetry slams, talent shows, youth symposiums, served as a keynote speaker, and began to mentor young students through the CTAG program. Many projected that by the time I graduated, I would be the poster child for the CTAG program as I was always at the forefront of whatever the CTAG program presented.

With all these organizations backing me, I began traveling to different programs and events across the country. Thankfully, my teachers would allow me to make up or turn in all of the work I missed. I traveled to some of the largest cities in the nation: Los Angeles, Washington D.C., Kansas City, Atlanta, Chicago, Indianapolis, St. Louis, Nashville, Montgomery, and many more, all free of charge. A lot of the time, I would even make money as I carried my business cards and poetry CDs in my bags. On these trips, I met, shook hands, and conversed with some of the world's most influential people such as, Susan Taylor, Spike Lee, Cicely Tyson, Bernice King, Julian Bond, Dr. Otis Moss Jr., Rev. James Lawson, Magic Johnson, and Marian Wright Edelman. Along my journey, I also met many prominent politicians and public figures. Thankfully, I had the wherewithal to know I was in the presence of greatness. These were the same individuals I had read about and researched. Whether it be in entertainment, academia, politics, economics, fashion, or athletics, these icons had achieved so much in every endeavor of human life. They were strong, intelligent, successful, wealthy, and beautiful people. More importantly for me, they were black! Do not get me wrong; I met amazing leaders from all races, ethnicities, and backgrounds and respected them equally. However, meeting those who looked like me meant the world to me. When I saw them, I saw myself because our stories connected. Anytime I had the opportunity to meet one of them, shake their hand, hug them, and embrace them - the new life I envisioned for myself became more realistic. With attentive ears, I listened to all they said and was outspoken when necessary. I even carried a small notepad and pen to take notes.

My most epic encounter was with Susan Taylor, Founder of Essence Magazine. Ms. Taylor had been hosting galas around the country to bring awareness to and raise funds for her National Cares Mentoring Program. When Dr. Kinney learned of her plans to host a gala in Cleveland, he knew we had to be a part of the action. Of course, we did not have tickets, but that did not stop us. All of the city's elite people and organizations would be there, and we had to be in the number. The tickets for the event were about $200 per seat, and a table of 10, would cost $2,000. I was making decent money from poetry but nowhere near enough to cover a table. So, we reverted to our old antics.

On the day of the gala, Dr. Kinney picked up two other students and me. We all wore the black and gold attire we received a few years prior to the trip to Morehouse. By this point, wearing professional attire was a norm for me, so I had acquired other suits. Nevertheless, we believed in uniformity, so I followed the dress code with a few adjustments to stand out. The event was held at one of the fanciest hotels in downtown Cleveland. The event security was tight, and for the first time ever, I witnessed Dr. Kinney be denied entry to an event. None of our normal schemes worked. The security officers and hotel staff did not care how nice we looked. We did not pay in advance for tickets, so they refused to let us in. Dr. Kinney pleaded with them for about twenty minutes, but they would not fold. For the first time, I saw disappointment rest on Dr. Kinney's face. As we left the hotel lobby, we were greeted by a gentleman who was obviously of high importance. I do not recall his name, who he was, or what he did. However, the custom Armani suit and AMG Mercedes Benz he left parked outside spoke for themselves. He walked swiftly and spoke to Dr. Kinney. Then, Dr. Kinney followed him past security to the elevator, and no one said a word. After reaching the elevator, Dr. Kinney gestured us to come along. I do not know how he pulled it off, but after that, I knew it was only due to the creator's grace that we were there. When the elevator stopped and opened, we were welcomed by a grand foyer with an exquisite chandelier hanging from the ceiling. Around the corner, people in fine clothing stood with cocktails in hand and appeared to be conversing about the most intriguing topics. As I ventured around the ballroom, I heard so many ideas and wealth tips. They discussed stocks, property, achievements, and excellence. I loved what I heard.

We did not have a table, so for an hour, we transitioned between the hallway and grand ballroom where the event was actually taking place. We would stick our head in and out of the door or stand in the back of the room to listen to all of the speeches. Ms. Susan Taylor's speech impressed me the most. She was so calm and free-spirited. She was passionate, insightful, and loving. This mentoring movement was something she genuinely cared about, and because of her sincerity, she won the crowd and made them care about it too.

When the event was over, Ms. Taylor hosted a meet and greet to shake hands and have small talk with the attendees of her very successful fundraising gala. The line to talk to Ms. Taylor was lengthy, and understandably so. Everyone wanted a piece of her wisdom and knowledge. I watched her closely as she spoke to everyone who came up to her. She was so graceful. By 10:30 PM, she still hadn't made it halfway through the line. Her staff announced, "Ms. Taylor would like to meet everyone, but she may not be able due to time constraints." Immediately, I grew frantic.

"We did not come all this way for nothing," I said. We were going to meet Susan Taylor. When her staff began to pack up, we jumped out of the line, walked to the front by her table, and stood there.

Ms. Taylor turned around, noticed us, and asked, "Why are you young men at my event so late in the evening?" We explained that we were high school students being mentored by Dr. Kinney, CTAG, and the B.R.I.C.K. Program. Ms. Taylor applauded us and told us to stay on the right path and that all would work in our favor. She hugged us and sent us on our way.

Before she walked away, I asked, "Ms. Taylor, do you mind if I perform a poem for you? It will only take a few minutes." She did not hesitate and ecstatically obliged. There were still a significant amount of people on the floor, so all eyes were on me. I positioned myself where everyone could see me, and I recited my poetry with conviction in my soul.

Giving Birth to the Future

I'm Pregnant

I know it's hard to believe, right?

It's driving me nuts

I have been hiding this from everyone for nine months, and at any time I could go into labor

I am a 16-year-old pregnant father and

I do not know how to act

How to react

How I had this transaction

However it occurred or however it happened

I'm Pregnant

And I may not have ovaries, you see

But I'm giving birth to my thoughts and my passions

My hopes and my dreams

The egg of knowledge is traveling down the fallopian tubes of my cerebral cortex

And impregnating my subconscious

Drawing and developing

Being nurtured by Imhotep, Aristotle, Louis Farrakhan, Malcolm X, and Dr. King

Because you see, I have a dream

I have been to the mountaintop

I have been to the Pennsylvania Alleghenies

I have been to the top of the hill

But you see, I may not make it

This pregnancy is making me yell!

This baby that I am nurturing that started as a simple stem cell

Has differentiated to the hope of the future that we can now all hail

But now it's getting hard

And I'm getting weak

And I do not think I can last much longer

But me thinking about this baby is just a steroid to make me stronger

But this is a larger task

What kind of responsibility has been placed on me

I'm just a 16-year-old child

How can I carry out this pregnancy

I need help from the community

It takes a village to raise a child

So I have to get information for this baby from whoever provides

I have an unusual taste of combinations for what feeds knowledge

How about a poor kid from Cleveland who attends Morehouse College

Who gets high off books with no narcotics

And this baby is just going up and down and up and down just like stock markets

Now listen, I may be the mother of this child

But his father will be the wisdom of history's trails

But you see, now it's getting hard again

And I'm starting to lose hope

It's hard for me to breathe

I can fill it in my throat

My baby will not survive

I'm quickly letting him go

But I have to remember that this baby is what three generations ahead have been waiting for

Even though I'm hurting

My feet are swollen, and I'm having hot flashes

I just wanna give birth to this million-pound baby

I'm sick of having distractions

The joy of the world is now in zion
But I'm not
My baby's stories has yet to be told
My baby is a dream
My baby is a vision
My baby's destiny is yet to unfold
I have so much passion developing in my belly that my abdomen
might explode
I'm giving birth to the future
I'm giving birth to future doctors and lawyers
I'm giving birth to the archaeologist and to the wildlife explorers
I'm giving birth to the millionaires and the architect designers
I'm giving birth to the landscapers and to the airplane pilots
I'm giving birth to the homeless
I'm giving birth to the free
I'm giving birth to more successful families
I'm giving birth to CMSD
I'm giving birth to a vision because Imam Jahmil and Emmett Till
birthed one for me
I'm giving birth to my community
I'm giving birth to my people
Giving birth is like Mel Gibson, a weapon that is lethal
Which makes me a lethal weapon
Now I see why women are so strong
Because giving birth is a painful blessing
I'm giving birth for my ancestors who were hung, shot, or choked
Awww man is this the baby
I know I ain't crazy
I think my water just broke
So once again I'm getting weak

And once again I'm having contractions

Oh this is the motherload

I think this time it's happening

So now I'm pushing and I'm pushing

And I'm huffing and I'm puffing

And I done forgot all about Lamaze class (wo)man

So now I'm just roughing

One push, two push…

Three push, four

My mind just gave birth to a vision

For the whole world to explore

This is a hard process

I just gave birth what more can I say

But it's not just me

Each and every one of us gets pregnant every day

But we are constantly killing our children

Murdering them before we even know their purpose

Killing our children is hurting America

Stop Having These Mental Abortions

So my baby's name is dream to vision

Her nickname is vision to reality

Together me and vision can change the world

With sights of change as our salary

With hardships as determination

And knowing that we can make a change is an obligation

So we all have to go out and make a difference

We all have to go out and make a stand

So in three generations our kids can feel like All State and know they're in good hands

You see we come from the dirt

So we have to be the promise
Because like TNT, baby we know drama
Just to inform you
The change did not begin or end with President Obama
And the war did not end when we found Osama
In all reality, Us, Glenville Tarblooders, needed those East High
Bombers
And no, it's not about chasing coins like your name was Sonic
It's about giving back
It's about the community
It's about determination
It's all about unity
But it took this baby to make this true to me
Please do not be offended people after I say it
But this is the only time I will encourage my young people to get
pregnant
So go and make a baby that you can adore
And give birth to a vision for the whole world to explore
I'm Pregnant

"Wow, what a concept! How did you come up with that?" she inquired. The truth was, just a few weeks prior, Dr. Kinney suggested that I wrote a poem about giving birth. I did not know much about having children, so we researched and talked about it. A few days later, boom — I had another hit poem on my hands. Ms. Taylor did not wait for my response. The question may have been rhetorical. She hugged me, placed her warm, soft hands around my round sweaty face, and kissed me gently on the cheek. She hugged me a few seconds longer and, while doing so, imparted wisdom that I remember verbatim to this day.

Ms. Taylor had denied photos all night. The poem got her so high in spirits that I think she forgot all about it. She insisted that one of her crew members take a photo of the two of us and a photo of our entire group. Dr. Kinney did not want to be in the photo. Even though he much as much a part of the experience as everyone else, he preferred to stay in the background. That's how I landed my first feature in Essence magazine. The magazine printed a section that included the photos and highlighted me, my mentors, and the B.R.I.C.K. program.

Considering everything I was involved in, Dr. Kinney believed I was on my way to being a top candidate to any school I wanted. I was involved in multiple extracurricular activities, and my grades were at an all-time high. Each grading period, I boasted 3.5, 3.7, and 3.9 GPAs. My cumulative grade point average had increased to 3.4, making me a high merit roll student.

The only college I wanted to attend was Morehouse, but I had no clue how I would afford it. After doing heavy research, I learned that attending Morehouse would be two times more expensive than attending my local state college. Also, Morehouse wasn't big on giving scholarship funds. My teachers and mentors encouraged me to look into other schools and not put all my eggs in one basket, just in case Morehouse did not work out. I refused to heed their advice. For a period of time, Morehouse College would be the only college to which I applied. Eventually, my guidance counselor, with the threat of punishment, forced me to complete the common applications. There were two separate common apps, both with the same intent. One was for predominantly white institutions (PWIs), and the other was for historically black colleges and universities (HBCUs). The catch was these applications only gave admissions access to certain public colleges in both sectors from around the country. Private Schools like Morehouse, Howard, and Spelman had to be applied to separately.

Choosing the right college was a big deal for me. I had visited many colleges and found many of them to be excellent institutions of higher learning. However, I wanted to be in a place where I felt seen, loved, nurtured, and respected. I wanted to feel like I mattered, and I did not receive those feelings standing on the campuses of large Division One and Division Two schools. Even though I visited other HBCUs, I did not feel the strong connection I felt when I stepped foot on the campus of Mother Morehouse.

The Morehouse College admissions application process was intense. The application alone was close to 40 pages. There were short answer questions, extended response questions, essay prompts, and literature. I worked tirelessly on the application. Day and night, I woke up, wrote essays, had them edited by teachers, and continued the cycle. Dr. Kinney was also a heavy critic of my application process. He would have me revise my essay several times before it was crafted to perfection. It took almost a full four weeks to complete the whole application. The application was probably the most work I had done on a single project in my entire life. I felt good about what I did. I had no doubt in my mind that I was going to get accepted. Once all my college applications were complete, I shifted my focus to how I would pay for my education at Morehouse.

I knew we were poor, but I did not know how poor until it was time to fill out financial aid information. Once I realized I would not have any assistance from my mom to help send me to college, I knew I had to get focused. I jumped into the scholarship hunt with the vigor of a mad man, and for most scholarship applications, I was the perfect candidate. Although it may have been stereotypical, the plight of my life was following the narrative of the young impoverished boy who came from nothing and made himself into something. I told the story of a young man raised by a single mother with three children growing up in an inner-city where crime and homicide were at high rates. I do not say this to glorify or make light of our situation, we had some really difficult times. But these were the types of stories Dr. Kinney and I knew people would look for, and it just so happened to be my real life.

I applied for just about every scholarship I discovered, even those I knew I would not qualify for. The hunt for scholarships was intense work, so Dr. Kinney gave me office space in one of his buildings. This ensured that I had access to a quiet space to think, WiFi, a printer, food, or anything else I needed. As the workload increased, I stayed with Dr. Kinney more. I was busier than most adults and had developed the resume of a 50-year-old man, too. As I completed applications, I realized that all the ripping and running over we had done over the last few years were for that very moment. Most of the scholarships inquired about community service, extracurriculars, leadership activities, hobbies, and awards. Most of them asked very little about academic performance. Thanks to my mentors, I was prepared, and on many occasions, I exceeded the scholarship's requirements. I would ultimately apply to over 40 scholarships in hopes of receiving funding for my future endeavors.

As my senior year rolled along, I found myself in the College Now, Greater Cleveland office often. This was our school's scholarship and college preparation office, where I spent the majority of my senior year. As seniors, we had lighter class loads than underclassmen. Whereas they did not dismiss until 2:30 PM and had a full block schedule, I would be done by 1:30 PM with a potential break or two in between classes. While many of my classmates left school, went home for the day, or slid to their favorite burger joint for lunch, I sat in the office. I wanted to know who had the scholarships and what was the most effective way for me to secure them.

Ms. Tiffani White and Ms. Denise Wiggins were the two scholarship coordinators who serviced our building, and they were extremely helpful. In many ways, they became mentors for me as well. They helped organize all of my scholarship information and were an outlet when I needed to vent about life. For my final year of school, the scholarship office was my safe space, and I never ever wanted to leave there. Very often, I had to be kicked out of the office and forced to go to class.

The spring semester of senior year rolled around faster than I expected, but all of my hard work was paying off. I was being accepted to so many colleges. Many of them offered me tuition scholarships to entice my decision. Every Monday morning, Ms. Bell, my high school principal, would take over the school's PA system and leave an inspiring message for the scholars that week. In her address, she would highlight students for their achievements in order of classification, and each class had an adjective to describe the cohort. There were Fantastic Freshmen, Super Sophomores, Jammin Juniors, and Sensational Seniors. Ms. Bell would highlight the school's athletic program and all of its accomplishments. I would love it when she announced the accomplishments of the seniors. She would highlight all the new colleges that scholars had been accepted to over the previous week. My name was always one of the ones mentioned for new accolades. In the College Now, Greater Cleveland office, it was no different. Each college acceptance letter was hung on the wall on a bulletin board in the back of the classroom. I had so many that Ms. White decided not to hang anymore until my Morehouse College acceptance letter came, so there would be room for all the students' college acceptance letters. Perry and several other students were also experiencing success, with college acceptance letters continuously rolling in.

Several weeks after the spring semester began, I still had not heard from Morehouse College. I grew anxious and began to check the mail religiously until a letter came. After receiving so many college acceptance letters, I had become familiar with the packaging — larger, heavier envelopes normally meant acceptance while smaller, lighter envelopes normally meant a rejection. One day, I walked into the house, and there was a letter sitting on the table. It had my name on it, and it bore the Morehouse trademarks. I was instantly afraid. I did not want to open the letter alone. So, I called my mother in the living room to assist. I had my mother pick up the envelope. The envelope was large but extremely lightweight. I did not know what to expect. Fearful, I took the envelope from my mother's hand and opened the package. The letter read something along the lines of:

"Dear Cedric,

Although we appreciate your interest in Morehouse College, at this time, we are currently considering other applicants for enrollment. Your application has been placed on the Wait List, and we will reach out to you if a position becomes available."

After reading the first few lines, I did not bother to read the rest. My mother stood in silence as she could see dissatisfaction spreading across my face. My feelings were hurt, and I was extremely disappointed with the results. I went to my room with my "waitlist paper" in hand and cried. I wanted to call Dr. Kinney, but I did not know how he would view me after receiving the news. The next morning, I did not feel like going to school. This may have been the first day I was extremely late without a legitimate excuse. Even though I was on campus, I did not attend one class. I went between Mr. Golden's office and the College Now office spreading the news. No one was more hurt about the situation than I was. Being waitlisted by a school like Morehouse more than likely meant you were not going to get in. But since I had been offered acceptance and tuition to many other schools across the country, no one in my school really saw the denial as a big deal. That day, I hated talking to my teachers, even Mr. Golden, as they all encouraged me to move on and look at my other options. Dogmatic and stubborn, that wasn't the answer I wanted to hear. After school that evening, I finally gathered the courage to inform Dr. Kinney.

"Waitlist?" Dr. Kinney asked after I told him the news.

"Exactly. The same thing I wondered." I responded.

"I do not understand," Dr. Kinney said with a slight chuckle of disbelief.

"I do not understand either. I did everything you said. I joined organizations. I did community service. I got good grades. How could I get waitlisted? I did all of this work for nothing," I rebutted.

"Not for nothing," Dr. Kinney responded. "We're going to figure this out. You're going to Morehouse." I was grateful Dr. Kinney did not have the same mentality as some of the people in my school. Being a proud alum of Morehouse, he understood the weight of my dilemma. "We are going to call and bug them and find out why you were waitlisted and what you could have done to be a better candidate." Dr. Kinney decided.

Over the next few days, Dr. Kinney and I made a game plan and included Mr. Roberts and Basheer. We would have as many people as possible to call the Morehouse admissions office to receive a definitive decision on my acceptance. "If they are going to deny you, they should just deny you." Dr. Kinney said. "This is like playing with people's emotions." He was right. I had never been more stressed in my life. Each day as we put the plan in place, I awaited a call, an email, a letter, but nothing came. My mentors called the school and received no solid information about my situation. Feeling defeated on the inside, unbeknownst to anyone else, I began to look at other options. In the heat of the moment, I began to doubt myself. I began to think I wasn't good enough to get into Morehouse College and become a Morehouse Man. Maybe I wasn't meant to be a Morehouse Man after all. I planned to attend one of the many colleges that accepted me and get over it, as so many had advised. This thought process made me feel better. That kind of talk made me feel better about not getting the information I wanted to receive. A conversation with my good friend, Alex, who had been accepted to Spelman College, motivated and reinvigorated me to pursue my dream.

Additionally, my mentors never gave up on me. Mr. Golden even got back on the Morehouse bandwagon with me when he found out I wasn't going to let it go. I was determined to fight it until the end. Until Morehouse officially told me that I was not accepted, I continued my pursuit. In the meantime, I continuously worked on scholarships, hoping to secure funds to cover the cost of school.

Weeks passed, but Dr. Kinney and my mentors continued to pressure Morehouse for an answer. On a warm spring Wednesday evening, a letter from Morehouse was delivered to my home. This time around, I was more skeptical than the first. I did not buy into the packaging ordeal or wait for my mother to open the letter. I was ready to know my fate — good or bad. I took the letter, went into my room, closed the door, and gawked at the envelope. I did not open it immediately. I loosened my tie, took off my dress shoes, and relaxed, preparing myself for whatever emotions would surface. I was overcome with emotions. I did not know how to think or feel. Maybe they would deny me for aggravating them so much, I thought to myself. Finally, after gaining enough resolve, I opened the letter, and it read:

"Congratulations....."

I do not know what the rest of the letter said because as soon as I read the first word, I jumped in the air, threw the paper, and ran out of my room screaming. I called out to my mother to tell her the good news. She was more excited than I was. That evening, I called everyone I knew that cared about my acceptance. I was so excited and could not wait until I arrived at school the next day to provide my letter to Ms.White. The next morning, I arose for school earlier than normal, eager to share the news with the school. No sooner than I had taken the acceptance letter to Ms. White's office, the news spread about the building — partially my own doing. I could not stop talking about it. Teachers came from all over the building to congratulate me. I was truly a celebrity that day. I beamed when teachers referred to me as "A Morehouse Man." They had called me that before, but on that day, it had new meaning. I was closer than ever to the goal I wanted to achieve, and I could feel it.

After reading the letter in its entirety, I knew to be expecting a financial aid package from Morehouse in a few weeks. Once again, I waited patiently, hoping that the news in the financial aid letter would be as great as the news I had received the day before.

Two weeks went by before the financial aid award letter came, and there was nothing special about the message inside the letter. Morehouse did not give me any scholarship money — not one red cent. The letter informed me of loans and a Pell grant, but those alone would not cover the cost for me to attend Morehouse. Also, I hadn't heard back from any of the scholarships for which I had applied. Once again, many of my teachers encouraged me to look at other options and go to a different school. The tunnel was again turning dark as the end of senior year was just a few months away.

This time around, I refused to give up on my goal. I reached into my bag of resources and consulted Dr. Kinney about formulating a plan to get the money I needed to go to Morehouse. Though I had done a lot already, I was willing to do whatever necessary to stand out more. Dr. Kinney came up with the bright idea to make an appeal package. The package would consist of a poetry CD, my speaker one sheet with all the engagements I attended, magazine articles, newspaper clippings, a fundraising DVD, the video from my trip to Morehouse College, and several reference letters from prominent people around the city of Cleveland, including Dr. Renee Willis, Chief of Transformation at CMSD. We also enlisted Dr. Otis Moss, Jr. to speak to some of the college administrators on my behalf. He was a legend at Morehouse and everywhere else in the world. He was a proud Morehouse Man who previously served on the Morehouse College Board of Trustees. What he said held weight, and when he talked, people listened.

A few weeks after our intense plan went into action, I still had not heard from Morehouse or any other scholarship provider. Although it was not apparent, I was under so much pressure. I refused to be made out to be a liar. For 3 ½ years, I made my claim on Morehouse, and I felt I had done all of the work necessary to be there. I did not understand why my journey was so difficult, but I was determined to forge ahead. I continued to visit the scholarship office and apply for more scholarships. One day, as I was in my AP English class, my cell phone rang. Initially, I did not move because I wanted to avoid getting in trouble for having an active cellular device during school hours. The phone rang loudly two more times. The teacher demanded that the phone be silenced immediately. I dug into the pockets of my slacks and retrieved the phone. I looked at the caller-id, and it displayed a number with a 404 area code. The phone stopped ringing, then began again. As I pondered who it could be, I realized 404 was an Atlanta area code. Who could be calling me from Atlanta in the middle of the day? I wondered. My spirit told me that I needed to answer the phone. I quickly raised my hand and asked to be dismissed from class. I made my teacher aware that it was an out of state call and could be extremely important. She allowed me to leave the class, and I ran into the hall to answer the phone.

"Hello!" I said.

A man with an extremely deep voice responded, "Hello, am I speaking with Cedric Thorbes?"

"Yes, sir," I responded.

The gentleman began to introduce himself and said that he served as the Director of Financial Aid at Morehouse College. "I received your appeal letter in the mail the other day, and I was thoroughly impressed," he said.

"Thank you, sir," I replied.

"You have done a lot of positive work in your community, and I feel that you deserve to become a Morehouse Man."

I grinned from ear to ear. "Yes, sir. Thank you," I replied again. We spoke briefly about my interactions with the NAACP and SCLC as youth president, as he was also a member of these organizations. We talked about politics and the plight of young black men. Then, he asked me the question I felt he had been waiting to ask me the entire conversation, "What is your relationship to the Rev. Dr. Otis Moss, Jr.?" I explained that in many ways, Mr. Moss served as a mentor and advisor to my mentors, and from being in their presence, I was given the opportunity to meet Dr. Moss, and he took a liking to me. I shared that Dr. Moss and I met with one another on different occasions to discuss my path to Morehouse.

After hearing my experience with Dr. Moss, he expressed his sentiments of Dr. Moss. The gentleman spoke of him with high regard and had the utmost respect for Dr. Moss and his contributions to Morehouse college and the greater world. He informed me that Dr. Moss had called on my behalf, and due to that phone call and my persistence with the appeals package, I would receive a $20,000 scholarship for tuition at Morehouse. My mouth dropped, and I immediately began to cry. I did not know what else to say, and my mouth would only form the words "thank you." Before he hung up the phone, he wished me well but let me know that I would have to be on my A-game to not bring disgrace upon Dr. Moss or the city of Cleveland during my time at Morehouse.

I hung up the phone and took off down the hallway with a loud scream. "Ahhhhhhh... Let's go!" I shouted. I could not believe it. I ran to the College Now office out of breath with tears running down my face.

"Cedric, what's wrong with you? Are you okay?" The directors asked. After gaining control of my emotions, I told them of the conversation I just had with the financial aid director from Morehouse.

"$20,000?!" Ms. White yelled. "Oh, my goodness! Wow, Cedric, that's really a blessing. You are really blessed!" she said. And blessed I was. After being awarded the tuition scholarship from Morehouse, I was no longer worried about how I would pay for school. I still had a large margin to cover, as Morehouse cost close to 50K a year. However, receiving that news gave me the motivation to continue forward.

After receiving the tuition scholarship from Morehouse, the rest of the scholarships started to pour in. It was like the floodgates had opened. Now all of my hard work was paying off for real. I won local scholarships, as well as some of the nation's most sought after awards. My scholarship achievements included The Coca-Cola Scholars Foundation Scholarship, scholarships from Omega Psi Phi and Kappa Alpha Psi Fraternities Inc., scholarships from Cleveland Metropolitan School District, College Now Greater Cleveland, the Cleveland Foundation, The Glenville HS Alumni Association, and a host of others. I even received a scholarship from the Boys and Girls Club of Greater Cleveland. Though I was not a club kid, Mr. Ron Soeder, the president, took a liking to me and gave me a scholarship. I also won another all-expenses-paid, week-long trip to Atlanta. No matter the amount, I was grateful as each scholarship got me closer to my goal. However, there is one scholarship I would win that took the cake.

In my senior AP English class, my teacher would make it a grade requirement for all of her students to participate in the Maltz Museum of Jewish Heritage Stop the Hate

Youth Speak Out Writing Contest. The winner would win a college scholarship. The scholarship prompt required you to talk about a time you faced some sort of prejudice or discrimination. In my lifetime, I experienced discrimination often, especially traveling across the country, attending events with some of the world's wealthiest people and their children.

Over the next several weeks, our teacher would require us to correct several drafts before our essays could be submitted. No one really wanted to write the essay, but as seniors, we could not afford to get an F on our report cards. In the midst of our essay writing process, something happened that boosted our morale. A representative from the Maltz Museum came to our school and held an informational with the class. She outlined the program, the essay competition, and gave us background on the museum and Jewish culture. There would be three place winners and seven honorable mentions. Third place would win $15,000, First-Runner Up: $25,000, and first place, a whopping $50,000 scholarship. The seven honorable mentions would also receive something. Now, everyone in the class was excited about submitting their essay. "Wow, a chance to win $50K. There is so much I could do with that money." I said to myself. I definitely would not have to worry about paying for Morehouse, but I knew it would not come easy. This was an AP honors English class. I would be in competition with the top scholars from my school as well as Cuyahoga County. Perry had his eyes set on the prize too, so I knew this would be a challenge.

I worked fiercely on the essay, just as I had done with the other scholarships before. I would retell the event of a speaking engagement I attended where I was greeted coldly by the white audience and had racial slurs spewed at me. It was a compelling story that only a few people knew about. After finishing the drafts of my essay, my English teacher encouraged me to change my essay but did not give a real reason as to why. I believe that the topic and rawness of the essay made her, in her white skin, feel uncomfortable. This is also the same teacher who asked why all the material I read was "so serious" back in 9th grade. After a constant debate over my essay topic, I refused and submitted the essay for grading and competition anyway. I would deal with whatever consequence came from refusing to change what I wrote. My English teacher gave me a B- and implied that I would not have any chance of winning the competition because my story was too stereotypical.

After waiting for weeks, we assumed none of us won and moved along. Honestly, there was so much happening in the final weeks of my senior year that I forgot about the essay competition.

One day, I received an envelope from the Maltz Museum announcing that my essay was selected, and I was invited to go to the next round as a semifinalist. I could not believe it. The letter gave me a heartfelt congratulations and commended me for being an agent for social change. The letter also outlined what would be required of the semifinalist in the final round. There were several other smaller requirements, such as a tour of the Maltz Museum, a photoshoot, and a lecture from the legendary Milton Maltz. Mr. Maltz, for many years, served as a broadcasting legend with his creation of the Marlite Communications Group. In his later years, he sold the company but still maintained a stronghold on the broadcasting industries. He was also the founder of the Maltz Museum of Jewish Heritage and a sponsor of the essay competition. In the auditorium of the Maltz Museum, Mr. Maltz outlined our requirements in the final round. In order to compete in the final round of the essay competition, we would have to stand in front of a room filled with hundreds of people and recite our essay on stage. The judges would factor in the content of our essays and our auditory performances to determine the winner. He gave us pro tips about using a microphone, making eye contact with the crowd, and exuding confidence while we spoke. He emphasized the importance of being familiar with the essay we wrote and the way that it read. The last thing he wanted was for someone to get up on stage and stumble over their words. His advice was solid, and coming from someone of his stature, I would follow it accordingly.

While others hated the idea of public speaking, I felt I had prepared for this moment my whole life. "I have spoken in front of many crowds in front of hundreds of people many times before," I said to myself. I had no fear of standing in front of people and speaking my mind. I felt more confident than ever about my chances in the competition. I was very competitive, so I would recite my essay day and night to ensure it read as fluently as possible.

Once the day of the competition came, I had converted the entire essay to memory. I would keep a copy in front of me, but I wanted to ensure I would be able to make as much eye contact with the crowd as possible. Besides, I knew from reciting poetry that the more familiar with the work I was, the more I could declaim it with presence. The organizers at the

Maltz Museum did not spare any expense when it came to the event. The event was held in Cleveland's famed Severance Hall, the home of the world-renowned Cleveland Orchestra. We entered the building from the University Circle entrance and walked into a hall full of people. People from all over the city were there, students, teachers, and family alike. There were lights, refreshments, and many prominent people from around the city at the event. Life-size cardboard cutouts of all of the semifinalists lined the foyer. I was amazed at what I was witnessing, but I had no time to take it all in as it was time for the contestants to head backstage. The show was getting ready to begin, and although confident in my abilities, butterflies began to settle in my abdomen.

On this particular day, I wore my best suit. Mr. Roberts had taken me suit shopping for this special occasion. It was my first four-piece suit. It was dark blue with light blue pinstripes and had a four-button waistcoat to match. I wore a powder blue necktie and a pair of black dress shoes. Standing in the mirror, I ensured I looked presentable and gave myself a small pep talk before walking on stage.

They gave us the order to sit in, which would also be the order in which we spoke. I do not recall my number, but I was somewhere in the middle. Those who went before me were good, really good. They attended some of the best schools from around the county; the competition was stiff. Finally, my name was called, and my heart dropped from my chest to the bottom of my feet. Nevertheless, it was showtime, and I did not have any time for fear. As I walked to the podium, I found comfort in seeing many familiar faces there to support me. My mother, my principal, Mr. Roberts, Dr. Kinney, and a host of others were there to cheer me on. The Master of Ceremonies welcomed me to the microphone. Before I spoke, he asked me a series of simple questions about myself, my aspirations, and my influences. His questions eased my nerves a little. After that, he walked away from the microphone. I stared into the bright lights that nearly made the crowd invisible, and I spoke:

"I felt like Dr. Martin Luther King Jr. standing in front of an angry, racist mob delivering a peace sermon. I looked into the crowd only to see rolling eyes and angry faces. Staring at facial expressions of aggression and anger, I did not feel welcome.

Placed on a panel discussion in southern Ohio, I was told to express my feelings about my high school experience. The majority of the audience was white. So were the four other students I sat on the panel with. I was third in line to speak. I waited my turn as the first two students went to the podium and delivered their speeches. As each finished, the crowd offered them thunderous applause. Now it was my turn. Nervously, I stood. The group in the front row shrank back into their seats. It seemed that they were frightened by me. As I walked over to the podium, people walked out. I knew it wasn't time for a bathroom break. My white counterparts did not receive the "walkout" treatment. As I began to speak, I heard chatter coming from the right corner of the room. I heard murmurs of the words "poor" and "nigger."

Rattled and confused, I finished my speech. There was absolute silence. I did not receive the roaring ovation that my white counterparts did. I went back to my seat, feeling underappreciated and useless. My presentation was well prepared. I could not understand why I did not receive applause from the crowd. Was it because I was black? Was it because I was from the inner city? I had no clue why they gave off this vibe. Being one of only six blacks in the room made me feel uneasy with this company. They showed they were not too fond of my being there. I had no idea why this discrimination and racism occurred. After my experience on the panel, my spirit was crushed. After witnessing the uncomforting audience, I felt that maybe they think one race is superior to the other.

Something had to change. I began to join organizations that pushed social justice. I am currently the president of the SCLC [Southern Christian Leadership Conference] Youth Division of Cleveland and The B.R.I.C.K. Program, which stands for Brotherhood, Respect, Intelligence, Conduct, and Knowledge. I am most proud of my presidency over the Cleveland NAACP Youth Council. As president, I speak out against injustice and for civil rights issues. From Cleveland to Chicago, from Washington, D.C., to Atlanta, I have held peace rallies and marches to stop bullying and discrimination. I hold protests to speak out against the injustices of the youth. For someone to be treated as unequal because of economic status or skin color is wrong. Dr. King said a man should be judged not by the color of his skin but the content of his character. So I will preach the sermons of justice and peace and speak out against discrimination so no other student will have to hear the silence of racism again."

The crowd erupted, and I received a standing ovation for my speech. I gave a bow, and I walked to my seat. The competition continued, and it seemed that every person who went got better and better. I had given it my everything, so no matter the outcome, I was satisfied. I did not end up winning the competition, but I was the first runner up and winner of a $25K scholarship. I was told that in my riveting speech, I channeled the likes of the Rev. Dr. Martin Luther King, which to this day, is still one of the highest praises I have ever received. Reflecting on that time, I think it was a great thing I did not come in first place. I would not have been able to turn down the $50K as easily as I turned down the $25K scholarship.

Although I was crowned one of the winners and presented with a large check in front of hundreds of people, the Maltz scholarship was only applicable to students who would attend schools in Ohio. Since I was going to Morehouse, the scholarship could not be used to cover the cost of my out-of-state studies. I would either have to stay in Ohio for school or forfeit $25K. I chose to do the latter.

My family and teachers pleaded with me not to turn down so much scholarship money. Even my mother began to change her tune about me going to Morehouse and thought, for a moment, it may be best for me to stay at home. I would not change my position. I had done so much to get this far. I could not let $25K change the direction of my vision. I would be going to Morehouse no matter what. People ridiculed me, called me crazy and stupid even for leaving all that money on the table. I did not care. I knew what I wanted.

Senior year rolled along, and as senior class president, I was stuck organizing our senior events. We held our senior luncheon, senior prom, senior breakfast, and several other functions. My favorite event was Senior Honor Day. This was the day before graduation, where all of the hard work of a scholar throughout their high school career was on display. Here, I would read the senior class prophecy, and teachers, faculty, and staff would give scholarships and awards to the top-performing seniors. On Senior Honor Day, I would receive over 20 scholarships and awards totaling around $200,000, and I would receive more scholarships and awards after. That year, I racked up over 30 scholarships and awards. I won more than half of what I applied for. I was truly fortunate, and all of the hard work I had put in had paid off. Morehouse was no longer a dream. With the help of my mentors and true determination, I willed my vision into existence, manifesting everything I ever wanted.

Senior Graduation came and went. It was the final step on a journey I set out to complete a few years prior. I ended high school and graduated at the top of my class. All I could have dreamed of was coming true. I was accepted to my dream school, and although I did not have a full ride, I was very close to paying little to nothing to attend.

Later in the month, during the summer, right before I headed to Atlanta, Dr. Kinney acquired office space in downtown Cleveland. The office was in Cleveland's Terminal Towers, which sat in the heart of the city. The building was owned by Forest City Enterprises, and Dr. Kinney was in close contact with one of the company's most powerful executives, Albert Ratner. Forest City was a family business that started in 1920. It started off as a small-time lumber company and transformed into a major realty trust, investing in hundreds of properties around the country.

Well, one day, Mr. Ratner told Dr. Kinney a story about

"some kid who went to Glenville who had turned down 25K to go to Morehouse." Dr. Kinney, with embarrassment, told Mr. Ratner that he knew me and served as my mentor. Mr. Ratner, intrigued by my decision to turn down the money, requested an audience with me. Dr. Kinney set up the meeting.

When I met with Mr. Ratner, I did not know who he was or his connection to the Maltz Museum. However, after a brief time, I learned that he and Milton Maltz were really good friends. Mr. Ratner questioned me about my decision to turn down the money and go to Morehouse. He thought I was a fool and told me to my face. However, I stood strong in my position and confidently told him that Morehouse would be the best fit for me and that I would be successful there. He asked me questions about Morehouse, its cost, and the gaps I had in financial aid. I had won a lot of scholarship money, but still not enough to cover all my expenses. I spoke candidly with Mr. Ratner about growing up poor and wanting to accomplish something that would make my mother proud. Eventually, after an intense discussion, Mr. Ratner sided with me. He took out his cell phone, made a phone call, and placed it on speaker. A woman answered.

"Hello," she said.

"Hey, this is Al Ratner calling to speak with Milton. Is he available?" he said.

"Hi, Mr.Ratner. Please hold for one second," she responded.

Mr. Maltz came to the phone.

"Albert?" he answered.

"Milly, how are you? How's business?" said Mr. Ratner

They gave each other brief catch-ups on life, and then it was back to the task at hand.

"Milton, I have Cedric Thorbes in my office. Do you remember Cedric? He's the kid who turned down the money." Mr. Ratner asked.

"Cedric, yes. Yes, I remember him very well." Mr. Maltz recalled.

"I have Cedric in my office right now, and he is still a few thousand short of attending Morehouse. Even though I think he should go to school here, I feel that I am going to help him and give him scholarship money to go. Are you willing to go half with me for his scholarship?"

Mr. Maltz agreed. Just like that, I had made more money from turning down the scholarship than I did from accepting it. Although Mr. Ratner deemed me crazy, I knew he respected my decisions. After getting to know Mr. Ratner well over the next several years, I knew that if the shoe were on the opposite foot, he would have made the same decision. I was a young man on a mission to accomplish a dream, and no amount of money would take the place of it. I would go on to attend Morehouse College, graduate with honors, and receive an award for being the highest-ranking academic scholar in my field of study. Mr. Ratner would continue to help me during my undergraduate career and even in my studies as a graduate student. As long as I would continue to perform well in school, he would have no problem assisting me with financial aid. His commitment has gone well past the $25K scholarship that I left behind, and I am forever grateful for his constant belief in me and his contribution to my cause.

WHY I WRITE

I do it for the one who created the land
For the man who carried his own cross to his grave
Where they drove stakes through his limbs
I send prayers to him
And he sends blessing to me
Through my ink pen
And when it sinked in that my purpose in life would be much
bigger than that of just running a ball or playing defense
I began to use these nouns and verbs to connect souls like
LinkedIn
And since I was the tier of the greatness of my race being
referred to as past tense, well
That's where my story begins
After my first big show in Cleveland, Ohio
Being interviewed by the masses
In an economy that was crashing
In an educational system where
Classes were not actually classes
But somehow, we were still passing
The reason I have to tell this story is because

This is why my caged bird sings
Just imagine a young boy age 15
Being asked questions about the state of young black
America
By a magazine
Baffled and humbled at the moment, of course, I said the
wrong things
And every since that day, I have begged, and I have prayed
that I'd have a chance to redeem
So Now
They've asked me why I write
And it used to be because when I put these words together, I
was nice
Painting with vocabulary vividly depicted
I used to write because my flow was prolific
I used to write because my style was different
Loud and boisterous
My words made Egyptian hieroglyphics look simple
Fighting back and forth with my rhyme scheme made my
lines clean
When I look back on why I used to write
I used to show my hindseen
But in hindsight
I used to write cause I was nice
Now I write to bring life and to bring light
I write to uplift more
I write to encourage a young man that it is more impactful to
pick up a pencil rather than a pistol
Because in this world
You only prosper if you're intellectually ready for war

I write to inspire my young people to soar
Young black ebony queen
You are more than just your assets
Your impact on life will be much greater than your fathers'
absence
For she was chosen by Horace
Her swarthy skin was a symbolism of hardship
However, forever lasting
The hue of her soul carried the darkness of an Egyptian
goddess
In a world that is covered by war, whores, and Warhols
In the bosom of riots and chaos, she remains a steadfast
apostle of Ma'at
Only willing to lift her fist if it perpetuated the idea of the
betterment for her people
Her bronze skin emphasized royalty
Her thick lips represent the ancestry of a people who traveled
the seven seas
Before Columbus could see
Before she was labeled a beast
Only if the Atlantic could speak
Her personality as golden as the apples that caught the eyes
of Atalanta
For she had virtue and principle
He womb has shed light to life's noblest men
I said her womb has shed light to life's noblest men
Lucy from which we have come
From the flesh of our bones to the dialect of tongue
Woman
From the nurturing of the soul to the nurturing of the son

Woman

And woman, it kills me to see what society has depicted you
to be

They say the apple doesn't fall too far from the tree

Well, the roots have been rotted

I said her roots have been rotted

Chains are still available for those picking cotton

For the bullets that struck Trayvon Martin

From the police officer who strangled Eric Garner

I ask our father

Why, as black and brown people, should we continue to try to
be great?

He said simply, "Son, just have faith."

PART EIGHT

THE POWER OF WORDS

My entire life has been consumed by words, and being outspoken helped to cultivate the life I envisioned for myself. The truth of the matter is, words saved my life. Whether consumed or spoken, those words have always been intricate in dictating my actions in the world. When I spoke negativity, negative things happened. I walked around, angry and upset without reason. I also did not know how to use my words to release any frustration I was feeling. I was in a lose, lose situation. I was not listening to anything positive to feed my spirit. I did not have an outlet to release the bad energy that was within.

However, as I grew older, I began to listen to the right people. I consumed knowledge that fed my spirit, and I began to lead a more positive life. As the words I spoke became more and more positive and uplifting, my life soon followed. From reading my story, you can see the direct correlation between the words I put in my poems and raps and the lifestyle I was living outside of them. They were practically identical! When giving lectures, I often say to people that I spoke the life I'm living today into existence. Everything I asked for, wrote in a poem, and continuously reiterated to myself and has turned out to be my real life. Also, the more I spoke, the more I gained a sense of self in the world. The world we live in is the world we create, and the world we create is the one we openly speak of. Of course, there's always work that has to be done. But the reality is that words are the single most important vehicles we use to create our reality. Without them, no idea or thought can ever be fully manifested. The more outspoken I became, the more I shaped the world around me.

Words are the most powerful tool known to man. They can be used to build a nation or tear down an empire. They are indeed our most useful and powerful assets as humans. Due to the powerful nature of words and their use, there is no room for spiteful, nasty diminishing self-talk. There is also no room for the harmful talk of others. We must always be conscious of our words and the ideas we project into the world. We must ensure that we use our words for good and the uplifting of spirits. The things we listen to, the things we say to others, and the things we say to ourselves directly reflect our true feelings about life. To be successful in this world, we must speak positively to ourselves and use our words to encourage others to grow.

The beautiful thing about words is that everyone uses them differently. There are over 7,000 spoken languages in the world, and they are all filled with words. Yet, the one thing that remains consistent across cultures and breaks language barriers is the power positive words can have on your life. I use the positives of spoken word poetry to articulate my position in the world. After I write, I read, internalize, and recite it over and over and over. However, I understand that everyone is not a poet. Here are three ways to ensure your word usage will keep you on an uplifting path, helping to maintain a positive and focused mindset.

Three Keys to Positivity

Read Positively I know this one sounds simple. But reading is one of the most essential skills necessary for a successful life. Reading can introduce you to a whole new world, and lifestyle you otherwise may have never known existed. The ideas we internalize from reading books help develop our thought process. Our thought process is what we project into the world. When reading, be sure to pick up positive literature that speaks to your spirit. Not saying every book you read has to have inspirational, but there should be a balance in the words you consume. Remember, your future is determined by the books you read.

Positive Friends are Best Friends. The second lesson is not as easy as the first. Good friends are hard to come by, and you could spend a lifetime searching for a good friend. But, the old saying of birds of a feather flock together still holds true. To live a positive, successful, and healthy life, we must be aware of the company we keep. More than any other single entity, friends can either hurt or help our futures. Most of this goes back to how we allow them to speak existence into our lives. Be sure to surround yourself with people who speak life into your being, who bring you positive energy and consistent love. Have friends who encourage you and promote your ideas. Also, have friends who hold you accountable when you step off the positive path. We must even become comfortable with losing old friends if the relationship is no longer fruitful. Being in a positive, healthy friendship requires a lot of time, trust, and sweat equity. If chosen correctly, your friends will help transcend you into another stratus sphere in life. Have positive friends and be cognizant of old friendships that no longer support your growth. Your five best friends will ultimately determine your future, so be mindful of those who you keep in your circle.

Positive Self Talk & Daily Affirmations With so many uncontrollable outside factors affecting our daily lives, it is crucial to be mindful of how we speak to ourselves. Many individuals in your life will have an opinion about you, good or bad. But that doesn't matter. The only thing that matters is how you truly feel about yourself. Most of what we feel about ourselves come from the things we say to ourselves when no one else is around or looking. This "self-talk" can make or break your confidence and deter you from many of life's opportunities if not used properly. Speak positively to yourself. The world around you is already harsh enough. Take a few moments a day to be nice to your inner self. Tell yourself you are confident and beautiful even on days when you do not feel that way. Post sticky notes of goals, aspirations, and dreams around your home so that at every turn, you are reminded of who you are and where you are headed. Write your goals down on paper and constantly recite them to yourself and others. Just because the affirmations are said allowed does not mean it can not constitute self-talk.

It is said that it takes 21 days to form a new habit and a little over two months to fully embrace a concept. Say the words and phrases listed below to yourself daily, and I guarantee that the words you speak will become your thoughts and begin to dictate your new actions in just a short time.

1. I am enough.
2. I am beautiful.
3. I am smart.
4. I am strong.
5. I am intelligent.
6. Today will be a great day.
7. I am worthy of my dreams.
8. I deserve to feel and look good.
9. I focus on what I want, and I get what I focus on.
10. I am grateful to be alive.
11. My life is a blessing.
12. Hard work and patience are the keys to success.
13. I will be successful.
14. I have everything I need to be successful.
15. My possibilities are endless.
16. I am worthy of love.
17. I can handle anything that comes my way.
18. I'm making everyday count.
19. Every day, I must wake up and work hard.
20. I love myself.
21. You got this.

WHO I AM

So they ask me who I am
A potential father, future husband, son, brother, educator,
friend
A man of many passions
Because the truth lies within
A brother lacking perfection
Living, learning, lessons
Chasing a life void of sin
Daddy was never around
So we quickly had to grow from boys to men
The only option was to win or lose
So we draw roadmaps to the wins
And to The Creator be the glory
Because 25 to life or dead before 25 was supposed to be my
story
But I'm about making my ancestors proud
So I'll fight for a better tomorrow
For sacrifices of the ones who came before me
And for the ones who come after
I just hope that there is no bigotry in their chapter

No injustice, no racism, no frienenemies in their pastures
More great nights out in the city
With less stick ups and give me these after
Less senseless killings, pharmaceutical billings, and corrupt
pastors
I question this country critically
And sadly I could not provide all the answers
Morally, economically, politically
The inner cities are still forgotten
Not physically, but mentally we're still shackled and picking
cotton
Inhale and exhale these words
I'm trying to get you high off 2nd hand knowledge
We're taking a trip to cloud nine, where the divine dine
And I'm your pilot
Every word departing from my teeth provides wisdom
The orthodontist could not prescribe it
With the ink pen, I'm lethal, and what I speak could have a
death sentence behind it
In the words of the late Nipsey Hussle
If I go before my time, I just wanna know if y'all riding or are
you hiding
In high school
They voted me most likely to succeed
Little did they know they planted a seed
A seed that will eventually reach the epitome of an oak tree
I'm just trying to achieve
In a world full of followers
I'm just trying to lead
And when it comes to fighting for my people

I'm black leather jacket
Afro the nappiest
Fist clenched in the air, Stockley
I'm float like a butterfly, sting like a bee because, in 2020, I
still live in a country that will ship me off to war
But will not fight for me
I'm Muhammed Ali
But sadly, in this B.I.G. world
It wasn't all dream
The only thing that matters from the time of your birth and
your death is the dash that's in between
So what legacy will you leave
What type of life will you lead
The nation is killing the masses
Consistently dropping caskets
America was sick well before Covid-19
And the virus is greed
Cash rules everything around me
No matter how many bodies come up missing in between
And if you do not know.... now you know capitalism is the
American dream
500 hundred years of oppression and unequal protection can
all be led back to revenue streams
Now we base our life's worth on Instagram likes and media
streams
My life's work is much more dynamic than what's presented
on a screen
Know what I mean
So I use my words as I evoke these psalms
My ink pen is my weapon, and I'll use it to try to write these

wrongs
A change gone come
But they bets not wait for long
I aspire to inspire before I expire
Do the great work before I'm gone
And when I'm gone
The lessons left behind shall live on
Every day I wake up and pray
And Black excellence is the norm
When I take a shot, follow through on the wrist
Keep the elbow tight
Perfection is the form
We need a space to speak
I speak, and the world is my forum
I'm blackity black and proud
To my people, I'm sworn
So I'm in it to the end
And my word is my bond
So they ask me who I am
I know myself as many things
To the oppressor, I'm a nuisance
To a slave, I'm the hope and the dream

MEET THE AUTHOR

"To have what average people do not have, I must do what average people will not do."

Basheer Jones

Cedric Thorbes is a native of Cleveland, Ohio and an emerging young leader in many cities around the country. Serving as an educator, public speaker, poet and author, Cedric has touched the lives of many throughout the nation. Cedric has received numerous awards and accolades for his dedication to scholarship, leadership and service. Cedric is a proud graduate of Morehouse College in Atlanta, GA where he graduated with honors and was designated "Top Ranking Scholar" in his academic field of study. Upon graduating from Morehouse, Cedric moved to Newark, NJ where he served as a teacher and received his teaching credentials from the Relay Graduate School of Education. Currently, Cedric serves as the president of the B.R.I.C.K. (Brotherhood, Respect, Intelligence, Conduct and Knowledge) Program and receiving a Master of Arts in Educational Leadership from Montclair State University . Cedric's love and passion for working with young people has led him to his life's work in the field of education. Cedric currently serves as a Vice Principal of Literature and Social Studies for a charter management organization in the city of Newark.

Cedric's goal is to provide every young person in the country with culturally responsive literature containing the social emotional components necessary to be successful in today's volatile racial and political climate. Working in some of the highest performing charter management networks in the country, Cedric has witnessed first hand the extreme need for culturally responsive learning. Cedric firmly believes "a young person will only strive to achieve what they can see" and it is our responsibility to provide the vividest images possible.

Cedric Thorbes has traveled to numerous cities across the nation encouraging young people to strive for excellence and to develop a sense of self. From his own personal testimony, Cedric provides examples of how to achieve success and maneuver through the obstacles of life. He aims to promote the importance of obtaining a quality of education. He challenges young people to take control of their lives and their futures. He lives by the mantra "To have what average people do not have, I must do what average people will not do." For these reasons, Cedric has dedicated his life to increasing the educational trajectory of young people around the nation.

STAY CONNECTED

Thank you for reading, OUTSPOKEN: The Memoir. Cedric looks forward to connecting with you. Here are a few ways you can connect with the author and stay updated on new releases, speaking engagements, products, and more.

FACEBOOK   Cedric Thorbes
INSTAGRAM   @kingthorbes @cedricthorbeslive
WEBSITE   www.cedricthorbes.com
EMAIL   cedricthorbes@gmail.com

Made in the USA
Monee, IL
12 February 2021